"T
of
be
and that's your own self."
Aldous Huxley

To my readers

Dear Friends:

Most people don't know what strategy is or how it works. Until a few years ago, I taught strategy exclusively to the leaders of the world's largest organizations. However, my focus was very narrow: using the rules of strategy for success in business.

Then I was diagnosed with a deadly form of cancer. As I went through treatment, I saw that many of my fellow patients were literally dying because they didn't know how to make basic strategic decisions. One of those who died was a dear friend who was the best man at our wedding.

In my own treatment, I was using the same decision-making tools that I had been teaching in my strategy classes, just in a different context. As I recovered, I realized how deeply every aspect of my life had been shaped by my understanding of strategy. Unconsciously, I had been using this tool all along to become a better spouse, a better parent, and a better member of my community. The principles of strategy had even strengthened my religious faith.

After my recovery, my life had a new purpose. My mission is now to share the 2,500-year-old secrets of strategy with everyone. I want to make those secrets easy for you to use every day of your life.

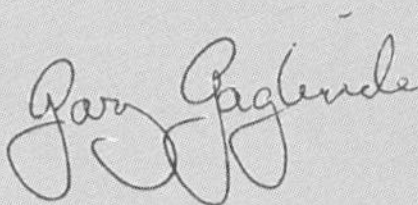

Published by
Clearbridge Publishing
FIRST EDITION

Printed in China.

Publisher's Cataloging-in-Publication Data

The golden key to strategy: everyday strategy for everybody, Gary Gagliardi
p. 192 cm. 23
ISBN 1-929194-36-6 (hbk.)
1. Strategy. 2. Philosophy. 3. Business management. 4. Military art and science.
I. Gagliardi, Gary 1951—. II. The Golden Key to Strategy
HF5438.5.S86 2005
658.8 /1 21 —dc21

Library of Congress Catalog Card Number: 2005900952

Clearbridge Publishing's books may be purchased for business, for any promotional use, or for special sales. Please contact:

Clearbridge Publishing
PO Box 33772, Seattle, WA 98133
Phone: (206)533-9357 Fax: (206)546-9756
www.clearbridge.com
info@clearbridge.com

THE GOLDEN KEY TO STRATEGY

Everyday Strategy for Everybody

HOW TO LISTEN→AIM→MOVE→CLAIM

By Gary Gagliardi

Illustrations by Steve Wright

Clearbridge Publishing

Other Books on Strategy
By Gary Gagliardi

Mastering Strategy Series

The Warrior's Apprentice

Sun Tzu's The Art of War Plus The Ancient Chinese Revealed

Sun Tzu's The Art of War Plus Its Amazing Secrets

The Warrior Class: 306 Lessons in Strategy

Career and Business Series

Sun Tzu's The Art of War Plus The Art of Career Building

The Art of Sales: Strategy for Salespeople

The Art of Management: Strategy for Leaders

Sun Tzu's The Art of War Plus Strategy for Sales Managers

Sun Tzu's The Art of War Plus The Art of Small Business

Sun Tzu's The Art of War Plus The Art of Marketing

Life Strategies Series

Sun Tzu's The Art of War Plus The Art of Love

Sun Tzu's The Art of War Plus The Art of Parenting Teens

Current Events Series

Sun Tzu's The Art of War Plus Strategy against Terror

Strategy has simple rules.

And it works so well because so few know those rules.

Get this book now and use strategy for the rest of your life.

Or don't buy it now and pay for it the rest of your life.

Dedicated to a loving Creator who
fills our universe with
opportunity and gives us all the
tools we need to harvest it.

The Legend of the Golden Key

- Strategy knows the stuff that stops you.
- Strategy gives the key to moving forward.
- Strategy gets you in touch with reality.

The Use of Tiny, Mysterious Symbols

Rather than explain the many connections among the elements of strategy, we use symbols to illustrate these relationships. You don't have to understand these details, but there is elegance in how it all fits together.

Five parts of a strategic position

Three levels of goals and rewards

Four steps to advance a position

Three concepts that define opportunity

Two ideas that create momentum

And Just So You Don't Get Bored

Explanation of Strategy

THE KEY PRINCIPLES

Personal Experiences

QUOTES OF WISDOM

Illustrative Jokes

Illustrative Stories

Rules to Games

Key Summary

Contents

Everyone locks up what is valuable, but people also lock up what is valuable in themselves.

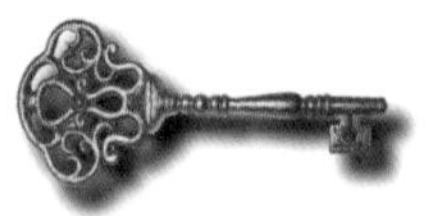

For every lock there is a key, but one key opens many locks. This key unlocks the potential within you.

Part I
Strategy, the Universal Tool

WHAT COURSE WILL TEACH
ME HOW TO GET RICH, FIND A
PERFECT MATE, MAKE MY DREAMS
COME TRUE, AND STOP MY
MOTHER FROM CRITICIZING ME?

STRATEGY

1
Life's Swiss Army Knife

Strategy is the handiest tool. It goes everywhere. It never wears out. It never goes out of style. It can open doors, start things, unlock treasures, fix problems, and make you look good no matter what the situation.

The purpose of this book is to change the way you see the world.

Tasks That Require Strategy

Strategy is useful in every aspect of your life. It isn't just for special occasions. It addresses problems that arise every day, but nothing is handier when you face a life-altering challenge.

In Your Personal Life

- ☑ Settling a fight with your spouse
- ☑ Any discussion with your teenager
- ☑ Working out problems with in-laws
- ☑ Dealing with a problem neighbor
- ☑ Kicking an addiction
- ☑ Knowing what to do when diagnosed with cancer
- ☑ Getting out and staying out of debt (or prison)
- ☑ Dealing with government bureaucrats
- ☑ Negotiating for a new car
- ☑ Getting upgraded to a better hotel room
- ☑ Investing for your retirement

In Your Public Life

- ☑ Placating an unhappy boss
- ☑ Raising money for your favorite charity
- ☑ Calling a truce with hostile co-workers
- ☑ Meeting people who can help you
- ☑ Getting out of work that poorly suits your skills
- ☑ Finding the career for which you were meant
- ☑ Organizing and motivating a group of people
- ☑ Getting the raise that you shouldn't have to ask for
- ☑ Recovering from a total, complete fiasco

Making Life Simpler and Easier

This list mostly describes longer-term campaigns, but strategy isn't about making more work for yourself. Using strategy means making your life easier. Strategy is a tool that makes even the smallest task simpler by leveraging the environment.

Strategy is about learning how other people's minds work and how that affects their behavior, and leveraging your knowledge to solve problems.

A man approached a very beautiful woman in a large shopping mall.

"I've lost my wife somewhere in this mall. Can you talk to me for a couple of minutes?" he requested.

"Why?" asked the woman.

"Because every time I talk to a beautiful woman my wife appears out of nowhere."

2
THE MOST ABUSED WORD IN ENGLISH

Strategy works so well because most people have no idea what strategy really is or how it functions. A million misconceptions separate how people use the word "strategy" from the science of strategy itself.

People say:

Strategy isn't what you **think...**

"I have been working out a strategy for refinancing the house."

"I thought of a brilliant new strategy for making money last night."

"My long-term strategy is to become an accountant."

"That was really a bad strategy when I spent that money instead of saving it."

"My strategy has been to keep a low profile."

But strategy is *not*:

- Another way of saying "a plan"
- Another way of saying "a good idea"
- Another way of saying "thinking about the future"
- Another way of saying "a choice"
- Another way of saying "a decision"

STRATEGY

Strategy *is*:

- A science based on the laws of human nature
- The way you analyze and advance positions
- A complete set of well-defined principles
- A method for making better decisions
- Responses adapted to specific situations
- A system for turning problems into opportunities
- A process of four steps—listen, aim, move, claim

THE KEY TO ADVANCE: **You need a practical system to advance your position over time.**

Strategy makes dreams come true by gradually improving positions. A "position" simply describes your relationship with other people in your public and private life. Dramatically advancing your position without using strategy is like climbing to a rooftop without a ladder. Strategy is the ladder you use to expand and improve your position.

Good things happen when you use strategy to improve your position. You gradually work yourself into a position that makes big opportunities possible.

Strategy is what you **do!**

"IT AIN'T SO MUCH THE THINGS WE DON'T KNOW THAT GET US IN TROUBLE. IT'S THE THINGS WE KNOW THAT AIN'T SO." WILL ROGERS

3
A Million Random Decisions

Every day, you make dozens of decisions. Over the course of the next ten or twenty years, you will make millions of decisions. Some of those decisions will seem large and others will appear small. However, a few years from now, many decisions that appeared big today will appear trivial, and a few decisions that seem very small today will turn out to have had a big impact on your life.

I was an aimless college dropout in my early twenties when I first started studying strategy. I had had four different jobs in four years, and I had been fired from a couple of them.

At the time, I had a problem with my boss, which was pretty common at that point in my life. Normally, I would not have known what to do, but strategy teaches that the first step in improving any situation is to listen. So I sought to learn more about my boss. In doing so, I discovered that he was very uncomfortable with computers. In the late 1970s, computers were changing many management jobs.

I was a salesperson at the time, but I had had some experience with computers in college, so I offered to help my boss with his computer reports. It was a small thing, but it changed my position with my boss in the way that I had hoped.

This decision had a dramatic impact on the course of my life. As the sales force's "computer expert," I was in a position to learn more about computers. In a few years, personal computers hit the market, and, seeing the opportunity, I found a job as a salesperson with the leading company selling those new computers. A few years after that, I started my own software company.

To make a long story short, much of the business success that I have had in life came from that small decision to help an unfriendly boss with his problems understanding computers.

How will the million decisions you make affect the course of your life? Most people go through life:

- Making decisions without direction
- Overlooking hidden opportunities
- Wasting time and effort
- Not getting credit for what they do

The Keys to Decision-Making

To make good decisions, you must:

- Know what your situation is
- Know what is worth your time
- Know how to make change easy
- Know how to get rewarded

The system of strategy clearly defines your situation, identifies potential opportunities, and points to the best opportunities. It also teaches you how to change your situation and get rewarded for it.

Make a good strategic decision now— **turn the page!**

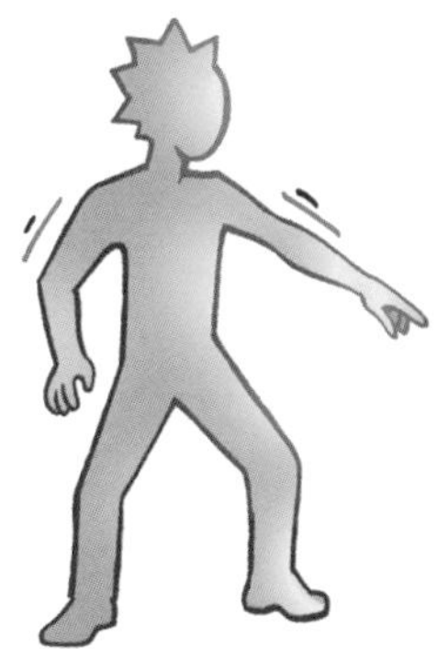

4 Why Our Instincts Stink

After people learn about what strategy is, they always say, "It is such common sense!"

They are wrong. Strategy makes sense once you learn it, but strategy often works contrary to common sense. Strategy works because its methods so often run against what people want to do in a given situation. Without training, most of our human instincts work against good strategy.

The Obvious Isn't Necessarily True

- ☑ The earth looks flat, but it isn't.
- ☑ The sun looks like it rises and sets, but it doesn't.
- ☑ The stars at night look tiny, but they are huge.

It took thousands of years for people to accept that the earth isn't flat, that the earth moves around the sun, and that the stars are huge.

Since you learned these facts as a child, you have no trouble accepting them. The problem is that no one studies strategy as a child. This is why people have so many strategic misconceptions. Over time, we all learn that the world works differently than we thought it did, but we learn from our mistakes. We come by those mistakes honestly. Most are based upon our instincts.

Children cry, run away, and fight.

Our instincts tell us, "Cry, run, or fight!"

All creatures are initially guided only by their instincts.

- The helpless young can only cry for others' aid.
- The skittish creatures can only run away.
- Those afraid of running can only stand and fight.

Because we are animals, our first instinct as children is to cry when we need something. As we get older and more capable, we develop the fight-or-flight reflex. When confronted with a challenge or threat, we either run away and hide or threaten conflict to discourage others from challenging us.

The good news is that, as human beings, we learn. By the time we are adults, most of what we do through the course of the day is learned. As we are trained, we automatically do what we are taught to do. The problem is that most people are not trained on how to face challenges.

THE KEY TO INSTINCT: **People react instinctually unless taught what actually works.**

After you learn how to use strategy, you know what to do when you meet a challenge. You will even seek out challenges, because progress comes from meeting challenges.

Successful people **use strategy!**

"DISCOVERY CONSISTS OF LOOKING AT THE SAME THING AS EVERYONE ELSE AND THINKING SOMETHING DIFFERENT." ALBERT SZENT-GYORGYI

5
ONE KEY TO RULE THEM ALL

One day, when I was about five years old, my mother was busy, so I slipped out through the kitchen to the garage. I got up on a chair to see what was on my dad's workbench.

A lock set with a knob on both ends sat there. Four screws normally held the handle on the door, but now they held the halves of the lock set together. I unscrewed the first screw. It came out after a few turns. I unscrewed the next screw, then the next and the next.

I was surprised when the lock set fell apart, opening like a book. One knob came off. At first, I was frightened that I had broken it, but as I looked more closely, I saw how it all fit. I could easily put it back together.

I looked at the parts inside. The knob had a long square pin that went through a hole in both halves. The other knob went on the other end of the pin. In the middle, the pin went through a square hole. When the knob turned, the square pin turned the piece with the square hole in it. One end of that piece pulled the latch in so the door would open. The other end of that piece was connected to a spring. When the knob was released, the spring pulled the lever back, turning the knob back and engaging the latch again.

There were only a few pieces. They fit together only one way. The shape of each piece made it move in a specific way.

Suddenly, I realized how simple machines were. In that instant, my world was transformed. In an "aha" moment, I saw in a completely new way how the world worked.

Strategy Is a Machine

Strategy is a mechanism, but like a child's puzzle it doesn't have a lot of complicated parts. Hidden inside, strategy has pieces. The pieces have shapes. The shapes fit together. Each piece has a purpose. Each piece works with other pieces.

For most people, the world of strategy is mysterious. People know the purpose and effect of strategy, but they can only guess at its parts. Because they cannot see how its parts work, they cannot use strategy effectively.

To Use Strategy You Must Know:

- Strategy's hidden parts
- What each part does
- How those parts work together

When you fail to make progress, it is not because something is blocking you. It is because you don't see your situation and all its parts.

Names are powerful things. Once you know what things are called, you can suddenly see them more clearly.

> "AN ORDINARY LIFE EXAMINED CLOSELY REVEALS ITSELF TO BE EXQUISITE AND COMPLICATED AND EXCEPTIONAL, SOMEHOW MANAGING TO BE BOTH HEROIC AND PLAIN." SUSAN ORLEAN

Once you start seeing the world strategically, your life is transformed forever.

STRATEGY

6
Knowing Where You Stand

Strategy is based on the idea that you have a unique place in the world. All your opportunities flow from that special position. From your point of view, your position doesn't look special. It looks like the most ordinary place in the world because it is the only life you know. Strategy teaches perspective, that is, a different way of seeing your situation.

Five Pieces of the Puzzle

When you open the puzzle box of strategy, the first five pieces that fall out are those that define strategic positions:

Strategy starts with examining the components of your existing position.

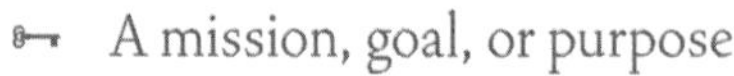

- A mission, goal, or purpose
- A ground where people interact
- A climate related to the ground
- The command of the individual
- A system for working with others

Mission is the higher purpose or goal that you share with other people.

Ground is where the contest takes place. It provides the prize you seek and defines the rules you play by.

Climate describes the trends that change your situation from moment to moment. Each ground has its own climate.

Command is the unique character that you bring to your situation—your individual abilities at decision-making.

Systems are the realm of methods and the skills that you master to work with other people.

Position Defines Relationships

If all this stuff about "strategic positions" is confusing, when you read "position" just think "relationship." You have a relationship with your property and the town you live in, but your most important relationships are with people you deal with every day. Human relationships exist in the human mind.

> THE KEY OF PERCEPTION: **Your position exists both in the physical environment and in the minds of others.**

When People Know You, What Do They Know?

You are more than a personality. You have a position. People know:

- What your goals are
- Where you stand
- What your patterns are
- What your character is
- What your skills are

> THE KEY TO POSITION: **You must see positions from five different perspectives.**

Strategy is a puzzle to most people.

7
WHAT DO YOU THINK YOU ARE DOING?

Strategy offers many techniques for taking advantage of opportunities, but the word "opportunity" makes sense only in the context of your mission or goals. For strategy to work, your mission cannot be completely selfish. Your strategic mission must be the shared purpose that unites you with other people.

Strategic **mission** defines the goals and rewards.

Strategic missions are pragmatic. No matter what you want out of life, you depend upon other people for your success. People support you only if you share a common purpose. This shared higher purpose defines the core of all strategic positions.

A man sees three men pounding on rocks. Because this man is a strategist, he is always interested in knowing what is changing. He asks the first man, "What are you doing?"

The first man responds, "I am earning a decent day's wages for a decent day's work."

This first answer tells the strategist a great deal about the first worker and his personal goals, but it still doesn't tell him what he wants to know. So he asks the next worker, "What are you doing?"

The second worker answers, "I am working to become the best stonemason I can be."

Since they are stonemasons, they must be building something, but the strategist still wants to know more, so he asks the third man, "What are you doing?"

The third man tells him, "I am building a cathedral, something that will stand for centuries and inspire generations of people long after I am gone."

For the strategist, only this last man had a mission that could unite him with every stranger walking down the road.

THE KEY TO MISSION: *What* **people do is less important than** *why* **they do it.**

The Three Levels of Mission

- People have economic goals.
- People have professional goals.
- People have philosophical goals.

The most basic mission is economic. We all share the need to survive with those we work with. Strategically, our place in the world determines our personal economics.

Strategic missions are shared to create unity.

Our professional mission makes us more valuable to others. Our skills are bigger than our immediate job.

The highest-level missions are philosophical. Philosophy brings people together over longer periods of time. These are the missions that people are willing to die for.

STRATEGY

8
The Race for Place

Ground is the physical part of your position defined by:

- The territory's ability to produce rewards
- Your ability to choose what territory to work

Strategic **ground** is where you win what you prize.

The ground is both what you own, where you are, and the roles you play in society. It is where you meet the competition and the prize you fight over.

Every Ground Has Its Own Rules

Every ground is unique. The only rules that apply everywhere are those of strategy.

A New York lawyer went bird hunting in Texas. He shot a duck, but it fell into a farmer's pasture. After the lawyer struggled through the fence, an old farmer drove up on his John Deere.

"What do you think you're doing?" asked the farmer.

The lawyer told him that he was going after a dead duck.

"This is my land," the Texan told him.

The indignant New Yorker responded, "I am an attorney and if you don't let me get my duck, I'll sue you."

The old Texan smiled and said, "That's not how we settle things in Texas. We use the Three Kick Rule."

The lawyer asked, "What is the Three Kick Rule?"

"Well, I kick you three times and then you can kick me three times. We take turns, back and forth, until one of us gives up."

"Why do you get to go first?" the lawyer asked.

"Because it's my land," the farmer explained.

The big attorney looked at the little, old farmer. Deciding he could easily win, he agreed to the contest.

The farmer's steel-toed work boot first hit in the lawyer's groin, dropping him to his knees. The farmer then kicked the man in the belly. The lawyer fell on his hands, throwing up. The farmer then kicked the lawyer's butt, launching him face-first into a warm cow pie.

The lawyer struggled to his feet, spitting out manure. When he could speak, he said threateningly, "Okay, now it's my turn!"

The old Texan smiled and said, "Naw, I give up. You can have the duck."

Choosing Your Ground

You must work the most fertile ground possible. Don't waste your efforts on barren ground. You want to choose ground:

- That is the easiest to work
- Where the rules favor you
- That offers meaningful rewards

THE KEY TO GROUND: **You must choose to put your efforts into fertile ground.**

Strategists must choose which ground offers an advantage.

"FIRST YOU SURVIVE. THEN YOU CHOOSE YOUR OWN GROUND. THEN YOU COUNTERATTACK." LOIS MCMASTER BUJOLD

STRATEGY

9
Doing Something About the Weather

Climate is the part of a position that creates change. Strategy works because time constantly changes the world. In the short term, these changes create a flow of opportunities. Over the long term, these changes give you time to accomplish almost anything.

The strategic **climate** must change with time.

The Pain of Time and Change

- People pretend the world is stable when it is not.
- All plans collide, so no one can predict what happens.
- When plans fail, people blame the plan, not change.

Change is the only constant. Your strategic position has change built into it. You must see how change is part of your position.

A daughter complained to her father about having to deal with all the changes in her life. Her father was a simple cook and didn't know how to answer her. Instead, he took her into his kitchen. He filled three pots with water and brought them to a boil. In the first pot, he put carrots, in the second, eggs, in the third, ground coffee beans. He let them boil. When they were done, he put them in three bowls.

"What do you see?" he asked her.

"Carrots, eggs, and coffee," his daughter replied.

"And how has the boiling water changed them?" he asked.

The daughter thought for a moment.

"The carrots were hard, but now they are soft," she observed. "But the eggs were the opposite. On the inside they were soft, but now they are hard."

"And the coffee beans?" her father asked.

"They weren't changed at all," the daughter observed. "Instead, the beans changed the water, making it into coffee."

"Those are your choices, my daughter," her father said. "Time can make you soft, or it can make you hard, or you can use it to change your surroundings. The only question is, do you want to be a carrot, an egg, or a coffee bean?"

THE KEY TO CLIMATE: **Climate cannot be controlled, but you can use its changes.**

Foresee Trends, Cycles, Patterns, and Reversals

- Every area has its own patterns.
- Every extreme creates its opposite.
- Wait for change if the current climate doesn't favor you.

Strategists use change as the source of opportunity.

Day follows night. Summer follows winter. If you have a problem with climate, you can either wait for it to change or you can move to a different place. You must be sensitive to the opportunities created by constant change.

10
Five Characters You Meet on Earth

The command you bring to your situation depends on your character. Some accept responsibility for their lives, but many let other people dictate their course. Giving command to others is just another way of running away from the challenges of life.

Your character gives you strategic **command**.

To understand any strategic position, you need to know who is in command and their character. Character can differ in infinite ways, but strategy focuses on five characteristics.

The Five Key Characteristics in Command

- People differ in how caring they are.
- People differ in how intelligent they are.
- People differ in how courageous they are.
- People differ in how disciplined they are.
- People differ in how trustworthy they are.

People behave according to their character. Given similar situations, different people react very differently because of the differences in their character. Character determines how they perceive their strategic position. The more you know about a person's character, the more accurately you can predict his or her behavior.

- Caring determines your dedication to your mission.
- Intelligence learns the rules of the ground.
- Courage faces the changes of climate.
- Discipline restricts excesses of command.
- Trustworthiness enables the cooperation of systems.

THE KEY TO COMMAND: **Your character determines the quality of your decisions.**

Weakness and Strength

One of the core principles of strategy—inversion—is that weakness arises from strength. This idea has many different uses in strategy, but, in terms of evaluating command and character, an overabundance of a characteristic is just as much of a problem as its absence. Recognize these excesses in yourself and your leaders.

- Excess caring is idealism.
- Excess intelligence is paralysis.
- Excess courage is fearlessness.
- Excess discipline is rigidity.
- Excess trustworthiness is oversensitivity.

Strategy teaches that an excess of any characteristic leads to weakness.

"LEADERSHIP IS A POTENT COMBINATION OF STRATEGY AND CHARACTER. BUT IF YOU MUST BE WITHOUT ONE, BE WITHOUT THE STRATEGY."
NORMAN SCHWARZKOPF

11
The Wow in Your Know-How

Our brains are not any more developed than those of our cave-dwelling ancestors. What separates our lifestyle today from theirs are the systems that we have built. Systems accumulate knowledge and skill and put them to work.

Systems combine separate skills into a strategic whole.

Systems connect an individual's skills with the skills of a larger group. Any respectable caveman could survive perfectly well alone, but our organizations today require us to work with other people.

Systems play a key role in defining any strategic position. You must know a group's systems and an individual's skills to complete the picture of their strategic position.

Two Key Systems

- Systems that support your mission
- Systems that advance your position

Systems Must Support Your Mission

Your mission points you toward the systems and skills you need. Since there are three levels to mission—the economic, professional, and philosophical—there are three different categories of mission-related systems.

Master systems that support your economic needs. This means identifying skills that will help you make more money.

Master systems to improve your professional abilities. This means specializing your skills in unique ways. Specialization makes you more valuable to others over time.

Finally, master systems that spread your philosophy.

The System of Strategy

Strategy is itself a system, a system for analyzing and advancing positions. The basic system was invented 2,500 years ago by an ancient Chinese general named Sun Tzu. Sun Tzu wrote a book describing the system of strategy called *The Art of War*. In Chinese, its name is *bing-fa*, which means "competitive systems." Everything in this book is based upon the ideas first written in this classic treatise on how strategy works.

Strategy requires systems to get people working together.

THE KEY TO SYSTEMS: **You must master the skills of working with other people.**

"STRATEGY IS A STYLE OF THINKING, A CONSCIOUS AND DELIBERATE PROCESS, AN INTENSIVE IMPLEMENTATION SYSTEM, THE SCIENCE OF ENSURING FUTURE SUCCESS."
PETE JOHNSON

12
Putting the Pieces Together

You now know all the pieces of strategy, but to get it working, you have to know to how assemble those pieces. We start with the five framework pieces that define a position.

> THE KEY OF COMPLEMENTARY OPPOSITES: **Strategic factors are two sides of a single coin.**

The Competitive Environment

Together, the ground and climate make up the strategic environment. They are complementary opposites. The ground is stable and physical, while the weather is constantly changing. You can control your place on the ground, but you cannot control the changes in the climate. Planning doesn't work because the environment is uncontrolled and unpredictable. Unlike planning, strategy leverages unpredictability.

The Competitive Unit

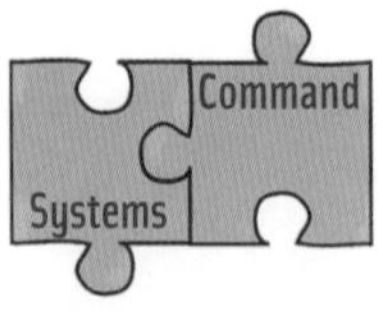

Systems and command are also complementary opposites. The decisions of command create systems, but individual decision-makers need systems and other people to execute their decisions. Leaders need groups and groups need leaders. Together, they make a competitive unit.

☯ Environments and competitors are joined opposites.

Mission Is the Key

Neither environments nor competitive units by themselves define a strategic position. A strategic position is a competitive unit within a competitive environment. What is the keystone of a position? What puts a specific competitor into a specific environment?

Mission is the catalyst that gives a competitive position its purpose. Without a mission—that is, without a goal—no position can be described as "strategic."

Mission ties together the ground, climate, systems, and command into a coherent whole. Like pieces of a puzzle, everything fits together only one logical way. The original Chinese for "mission" is *tao*, which means "the way."

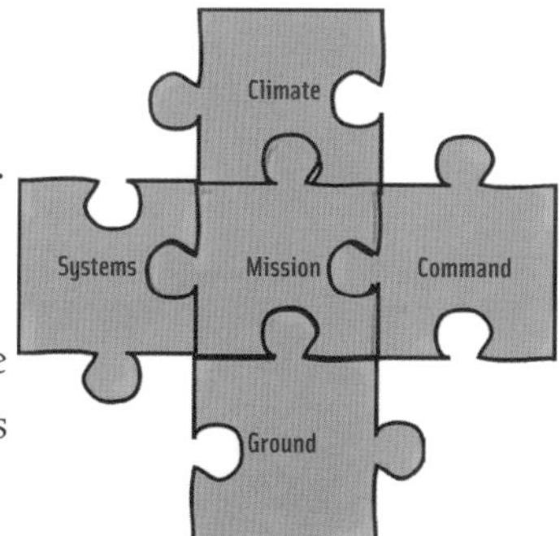

The Framework of Strategy

These five pieces make up a strategic position. This is the framework for all strategy. Most other aspects of strategy are defined in the context of these five components. An incomplete understanding of strategic positions arises when you overlook any of these pieces.

You need to know not only your position but the positions of all those around you who can affect your future.

> "THE ESSENTIAL ELEMENT OF SUCCESSFUL STRATEGY IS THAT IT DERIVES ITS SUCCESS FROM THE DIFFERENCES BETWEEN COMPETITORS WITH A CONSEQUENT DIFFERENCE IN THEIR BEHAVIOR." BRUCE HENDERSON

13 WHY LIFE NEVER GOES AS PLANNED

On the surface, planning and strategy look similar because they both deal with the future and have a goal. If you learn anything from this book, learn this:

PLANNING IS NOT STRATEGY!

- Planning works in controlled environments.
- Planning has specific goals.
- Strategy works in contested environments.
- Strategy has a general mission.

You can plan to bake a cake. Baking a cake takes place in a controlled environment, your kitchen, where you are master of your domain. You cannot plan to make a million dollars. You make a million dollars only where you compete against billions of people.

You can plan to paint a house. Painting a house is a specific task with a known list of ingredients (paint, brushes, rollers, etc.) and a to-do list (open the paint can, pour out some paint, etc.). You cannot plan to fall in love. Falling in love is a general mission without any known list of ingredients or specific procedures. Without specifics, you cannot tell if events arise out of a plan or a strategy.

THE KEY TO OPPORTUNITY: **You can only leverage opportunities created by others.**

Birth and Death in Contested Environments

Unlike controlled environments, contested environments are continually reshaped by competition. The change of climate creates new generations of command. New decision-makers create new systems. New systems create new ground, enabling explorers to discover new worlds, both literally and figuratively. Every field of science, industry, sport, and entertainment today was created by systems once unknown.

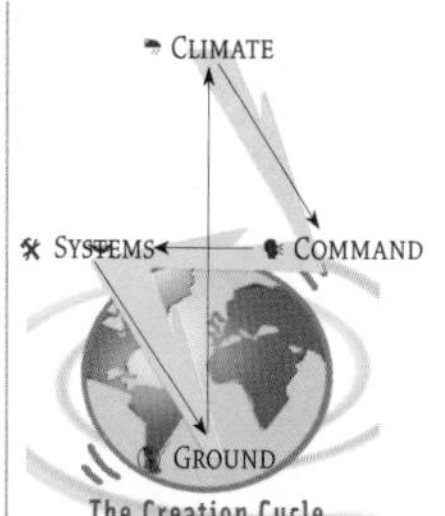

The Creation Cycle

Strategic climate is a pattern of change.

> THE KEY OF CREATION: **New positions are constantly being created by change.**

As the environment expands with our knowledge, the pace of change speeds up as well. Our descendants will explore dimensions, planets, and ground that we cannot imagine today.

The Race Against Time

In every adventure movie, there is an obligatory scene in which the hero outraces destruction by staying one step ahead of an exploding bomb, a rolling boulder, a crashing plane, a driving sandstorm, or a falling bridge. What most people don't realize is that their position in real life is similarly threatened. The forces of change destroy everything in their path and are coming after you.

> THE KEY OF DESTRUCTION: **Old positions are constantly being degraded by change.**

STRATEGY

14 THE FIRST KEYS TO STRATEGY

- Strategy is a process for improving your position in a challenge pitting you against other people.
- If you do not practice strategy, your instincts will repeatedly destroy your chances at success.
- To understand strategy, you must know what its parts are and how they work together.
- A strategic position is made up of five parts: a mission, the ground, the climate, command, and systems.
- Your mission is the core of your strategy, giving a meaningful context to everything else.
- The ground is the source of rewards and where you meet other people, contesting for those rewards.
- The climate is the uncontrollable force of change that destroys old ground and creates new opportunities.
- Command is your ability to make decisions based upon your individual character.
- Systems are methods and skills of working with other people to fulfill your shared mission.

Part II
Progress Advances Your Position

"TECH STOCKS DROPPED TODAY ON THE NEWS THAT TECHNOLOGY ISN'T THE SOLUTION TO EVERYTHING AFTER ALL."

PROGRESS

15
THE LAZY, RELENTLESS ADVANCE

Progress is constant improvement. Strategy continuously advances your standing. However, this relentless advance cannot be a grind. Just the opposite. The whole point of strategy is to make progress easy and fun. Forcing an advance just destroys you.

Using the Power of Opposites

To make progress easy, you put together complementary opposites (☯) in every part of your life. To be complete, a career must balance with a home life. Work gets more done when it includes play. Serious ideas are more powerful with laughter. Problems are opportunities. Tragedies have room for celebration.

Two drivers, a man and a woman, got in a car wreck. Both of their vehicles were destroyed, and they were both badly shaken, but fortunately no one was hurt.

"This is terrible, but we should be thankful that we are alright," said the woman. "I have a bottle of wine in my car. Let's celebrate and have a drink to calm our nerves."

The woman got the bottle out of the car and handed it to the man. The man took a big drink and handed it back to the woman. The woman closed the bottle and put it down.

The man asked, "Aren't you going to take a drink?"

The woman cleverly replied, "Not just right now. I think I'll just wait for the cops to get here."

PROGRESS

Changing for the Better

Alternating between different opposites makes progress faster and easier than exclusively grinding out one half of the equation. Advancing your position moves among:

- Joining others in shared goals
- Gaining more physical authority and responsibility
- Changing people's perceptions of change
- Increasing the trust of others in your leadership
- Developing more skills and interdependencies

The behavior of other people is compared to your own. You are judged both on what you do and on what you do not do. You advance your position and change your relationships by:

- Increasing your knowledge
- Focusing on what counts and avoiding distractions
- Finishing what you start
- Getting recognition for your achievements

Your position includes what you know and what you don't; what you decide and what you decide against; what you do and refuse to do; what you consider an accomplishment and what you consider a failure.

The purpose of strategy is to make advancing easy.

> "IF YOU WISH IN THIS WORLD TO ADVANCE, YOUR MERITS YOU'RE BOUND TO ENHANCE; YOU MUST STIR IT AND STUMP IT, AND BLOW YOUR OWN TRUMPET, OR TRUST ME, YOU HAVEN'T A CHANCE." W. S. GILBERT

16
Even a Child Can Do It

Every child knows how to play tic-tac-toe, but most children don't realize that tic-tac-toe teaches some of the most important rules in strategy. The basic ideas of advancing your position are no more complicated than the principles of tic-tac-toe.

Strategic positioning is as easy as tic-tac-toe.

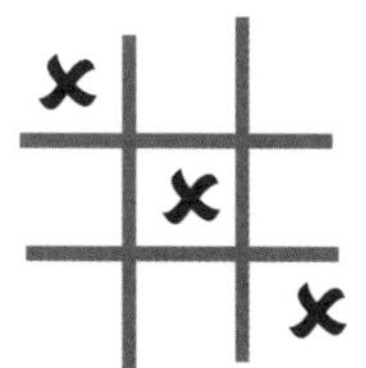

- Move to positions with more options.
- Adjust to the moves of others.
- Move instantly into openings.

Soon after learning the rules of tic-tac-toe, you discover that winning is based on positioning. The center and the corners are stronger than other positions because they offer more options, allowing you to move in three directions instead of only two.

A better position is defined by its future potential. Positions that offer you more options are inherently better.

Moving to the corners and center only works when you don't have to adjust to your opponent's moves. Blocking opponents from winning is more important than developing your own position.

Strategy requires that you first think defensively before moving forward. Doctors have the Hippocratic oath, "First, do no harm." Strategy has a defensive rule, "First, leave no openings for attack."

In tic-tac-toe, you wait for your opponent to make a mistake. Without a mistake, you cannot win, only tie. After a mistake, you must exploit that opening on your next move.

Strategy cautions patience in waiting for an opening because you cannot create opportunities for yourself. The environment is too big and chaotic. You must use the rules of nature, not fight them.

A teacher asked a computer student to explain the problems with his project.

"I am training a randomly wired neural net to play tic-tac-toe," explained the student.

"Why wire randomly?" asked the teacher.

"So the computer won't have any preconceptions about how to play," said the student.

The teacher shut her eyes.

"Why close your eyes?" he asked.

"So the room will be empty," explained the teacher.

Closing your eyes doesn't change the way the world works. Life is chaos, but its chaos isn't random. It is just beyond our control and complete understanding. Its nature creates rules. We can understand enough of those rules to avoid the wrong moves and meet the challenges we face.

Strategy avoids the wrong moves to win the game.

"HALF THIS GAME IS 90% MENTAL."
DANNY OZARK

PROGRESS

17
Pride Is Expensive; Progress Is Cheap

All progress depends on this:

THE KEY TO SUCCESS:

Success means making advances that pay!

You cannot improve your position by weakening it. If an advance costs more in time and effort than it returns in value, that advance weakens your position. Every day people take actions that cost them much more than those moves can ever return in value.

More Options From Limited Resources

Winning positions are those that give you the most options. If a move enriches you, it gives you more resources and more options. If a move is costly, it takes away resources and options. To make progress you need to get the best possible value for your time, effort, and resources.

Strategy teaches that every decision has a cost, at least in time.

Your resources are limited. You only have so much time, energy, and brain cells. Every decision you make steals resources. Without understanding the mechanics of strategy, you can work harder and harder and get poorer and poorer. When you choose your moves strategically, you leverage the benefits of each move to reduce the costs of future moves. You grow richer with each move in terms of the options available to you.

The Success Myth

The biggest success myth is, "You have to spend money to make money." Anyone can throw money or resources at a problem, but when you throw resources at a problem without using the tools of strategy, you dig a deeper hole for yourself. People don't know how to stop digging because they don't know what else to do.

Strategy Is Built for Uncertainty

Since you cannot know the future for certain, you cannot perfectly predict either the costs of or return on any single attempt to advance your position. When you use strategy, you are working the odds over the long term. Every advance is calculated to make eventual success inevitable.

You don't have to win every time in order to be successful. You only have to win more often than the average Joe. Given that the average Joe knows nothing about how to calculate the best possible advances, success need not be a matter of luck.

To win at all, you must know how to claim your reward.

> "TAKE CALCULATED RISKS. THAT IS QUITE DIFFERENT FROM BEING RASH."
> GEORGE S. PATTON

Good strategy increases your resources rather than destroying them.

18
The Mechanics of Manufacturing Luck

The components of strategy fit together into a machine. This machine manufactures luck, making life easy. We complete this machine by adding its moving parts.

- **Listen** to uncover new opportunities.
- **Aim** to focus on the best possible opportunity.
- **Move** to take advantage of opportunity.
- **Claim** to get the reward from opportunity.

The Progress Cycle

These four steps form the Progress Cycle. Without completing this cycle, you don't make progress. Listening without an aim is just curiosity. Aiming without moving is just dreaming. Moving without claiming is just dancing. Not completing the Progress Cycle is like building 90 percent of a bridge: a lot of work that doesn't get you anywhere.

> THE KEY TO THE CYCLE: **You must complete every step in the cycle to make progress.**

Progress is a mystery to most people, like the man on a flight from Los Angeles to Tokyo. About halfway there, over the middle of the Pacific, the captain announced, "One of the engines has failed and the flight will be an hour longer. But don't worry—we have three engines left."

An hour later, the captain announced, "Another engine has failed and the flight will be two hours longer. But don't worry—we have two engines left."

Two hours later the captain announced, "A third engine has failed and the flight will be three hours longer. But don't worry—we still have one good engine."

The man complained to the woman next to him, "This is crazy! If we lose that last engine, we'll be up here the whole day!"

The Complete Picture

The strategy machine works when you get all the pieces in place. When each activity is connected in the right place within the framework of a strategic position, its true meaning becomes clearer.

Listening connects us to the ground, that is, to our place in the strategic environment. Listening gives us command.

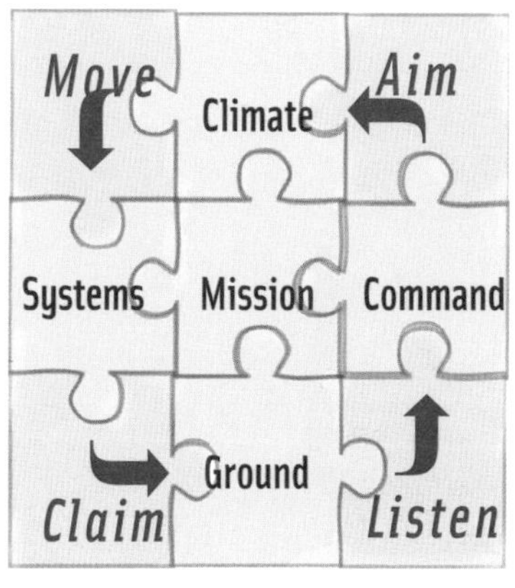

Aiming arises from our abilities of command, and it connects us to future changes in the climate.

Moving comes from changes in climate, and it is also connected to systems of working together with other people.

Claiming grows out of systems of working together, but it redefines the competitive ground.

PROGRESS

19 Master the Power of the Machine

The power of the Progress Cycle comes from repeating its use over and over again.

> THE KEY OF REPETITION: **The cycle gains power with each repetition and the speed of each repetition.**

Progress Cycles Big and Small

The four steps of progress take many forms, large and small, in long campaigns and in each small decision. On the largest scale, your life should one big Progress Cycle. In childhood you focus on listening. As a teen, you start developing aim. As an adult, you start to move. By middle age, you know how to make good claims.

On a middle scale are campaigns, which are a series of connected advances aimed at long-term goals. A campaign is its own cycle beginning with listening and ending with a claim. For example, going to college and graduating is a campaign.

Each step in the Progress Cycle can be reduced to a smaller cycle. When you listen, for example, something you hear draws your attention. When you aim to learn more, you move closer to hear. You then make a claim by asking a question. This ability to break down steps into smaller cycles is invaluable in strategy.

THE KEY OF SCALABILITY: **Each step in the cycle can be broken down into smaller cycles.**

Progress by Any Name Is Sweet

The Progress Cycle is a natural process. Sun Tzu, 2,500 years ago, called its steps *zhi, tian, hong,* and *xing,* meaning "to learn," "to foresee," "to march," and "to form," applying them to military success. In the scientific world, the Progress Cycle is called the scientific method. The four steps are called "observation," "hypothesis," "experimentation," and "evaluation."

The Progress Cycle can be cut up different ways, into more or fewer steps, but every part of the process must be completed to get the most out of advancing your position.

Debating about divisions or names for these steps is like the man who ordered pizza. When asked if he wanted it cut up into six slices or four, he said, "Make it four. I don't think I could eat six."

"EVERY DAY YOU MAY MAKE PROGRESS. EVERY STEP MAY BE FRUITFUL. YET THERE WILL STRETCH OUT BEFORE YOU AN EVER-LENGTHENING, EVER-ASCENDING, EVER-IMPROVING PATH. YOU KNOW YOU WILL NEVER GET TO THE END OF THE JOURNEY. BUT THIS, SO FAR FROM DISCOURAGING, ONLY ADDS TO THE JOY AND GLORY OF THE CLIMB." SIR WINSTON CHURCHILL

Strategy is a science. Some scientific words for listen, aim, move, claim:
- *Observe*
- *Hypothesize*
- *Experiment*
- *Evaluate*

PROGRESS

20
The Long and Winding Road

Ideally, you can get closer to your goals one small step at a time, keeping as many options open as possible. However, because obstacles block your way, you often must choose between different paths, committing yourself to a longer course of moves down a certain road. In strategy, we call these paths "campaigns."

Campaigns

Campaigns are necessary because life is full of obstacles. At critical points you must make a long-term commitment to get where you are going

> THE KEY TO CAMPAIGNS: **Multistep advances are necessary to go around major obstacles.**

For example, one obstacle to career advancement might be your education. In foreseeing that obstacle, you have to choose: do I go back to school or do I find another way around this obstacle? If you choose the path of education, you are locked into the path for a period of time. Campaigns are:

- ☑ A serious commitment of time and energy
- ☑ Undertaken only when clearly necessary
- ☑ Created only to serve your mission
- ☑ Steps that lead easily from one to another
- ☑ Their own clear standard of progress

Many people waste a good portion of their lives because they commit to meaningless campaigns. A campaign is like crossing an icy river by jumping from one ice floe to the next. You only choose that course if there is no safer way to move toward your goal.

Strategy sometimes requires a campaign.

PROGRESS

On the bank of an icy river, you cannot select each block of ice for your crossing. Situations change too quickly. You judge only the general conditions. Are the steps large enough to support you? Can you get from one to another safely? Only after you judge that the general conditions are good enough to make a crossing do you make a commitment to a campaign.

I was a successful manager in a large consumer products company, but I knew that I wanted to start my own company. The consumer products arena was too large, expensive, and stable to create any real opportunities for a private start-up.

I saw a path around this obstacle from my work with computers. The new market in personal computers would offer lots of new opportunities. I left my high-paying sales management job with Bic Pen to work as a salesperson in a Radio Shack store, selling little TRS-80s computers at minimum wage.

It was a new campaign, but not a risky one because I knew what my skills were. In less than a year, I was managing a Radio Shack computer store. Less than a year after that, I was a major accounts marketing manager. Less than a year after that, I started my own computer consulting firm. It took ten years to equal the salary I left at Bic, but by then my company was worth millions.

21
All the Directions of Progress

Progress will mean many different things during the course of your lifetime. Taken from the three levels of mission, there are generally three ways to look at how you can improve your position:

- Physical progress
- Intellectual progress
- Spiritual progress

Physical Progress

Physical progress is the most basic form of advance. It can take many forms. It increases financial advances, improvements in housing, or getting your body in better shape. Physical progress comes from:

- Expanding and improving the arenas you are in
- Building and perfecting your techniques
- Making more and better claims

Intellectual Progress

Intellectual progress is middle-level progress. It includes building up your knowledge, foreseeing trends and patterns, or building up relationships with people. Intellectual progress comes from:

- Learning and recognizing valuable information
- Developing an intense focus
- Adding good habits and eliminating bad habits

Spiritual Progress

It would be politically correct to call this "psychological progress," but psychology has become the opposite of strategy—a grab bag of excuses for why you are not advancing. Building up your spirit is the most powerful form of progress of all. A strong spirit is unconquerable. Spiritual progress comes from:

- Honoring your commitments
- Thinking about the future
- Raising and broadening mission

The Strategy Map

The relationships among the key elements of strategy create a mental map of your strategic position. This Strategy Map gives you a visual guide to the various ways you can build up your position and make progress. In most ways, these concepts of strategy are best explained by their interrelationships and how they work together.

The Strategy Map

> "THE REASONABLE MAN ADAPTS HIMSELF TO THE WORLD; THE UNREASONABLE ONE PERSISTS IN TRYING TO ADAPT THE WORLD TO HIMSELF. THEREFORE ALL PROGRESS DEPENDS ON THE UNREASONABLE MAN." GEORGE BERNARD SHAW

PROGRESS

22
Listen to Map Your Position

Listening is the first step because you need to know the territory before you can decide where you can go. To make strategy work you need to put all the information related to your situation into perspective.

Strategy teaches you a better way to **listen**.

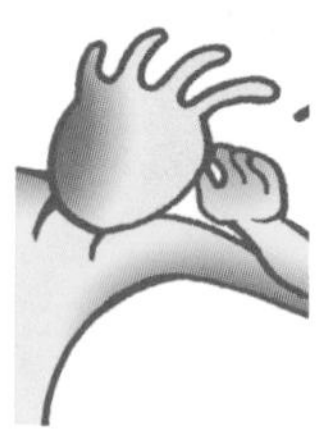

The Key to Listening: Only people can tell you about relevant strategic positions.

Skilled listening identifies how people see you and how they see each other. Listening puts each piece of information in its proper place. The goal is to understand the perceptions that define your position in the minds of the people around you.

You must know how to put all the information you gather into proper perspective. This requires knowing how to ask questions, question answers, and put every whisper you hear into a larger framework that makes strategic sense.

Making Listening into a Game

Listening is the most difficult skill for most people to master because they think they already know how to do it. We all learn how to listen as children, but as we go through school, listening becomes more and more painful. To make listening more fun and easier, we will introduce you to a number of listening games. These games allow you to collect the information you need.

Several pitfalls of listening are illustrated in the story of a U.S. senator on a junket to Europe who asked the Queen of England how she judges the people with whom she works.

"By asking them the right questions," said the Queen. "Allow me to demonstrate."

She phoned her prime minister and asked, "Please answer this question: Your mother has a child, and your father has a child, and this child is not your brother or sister. Who is that child?"

The prime minister responded, "It's me, ma'am."

"Did you see how that worked, Senator?" asked the Queen.

"Yes, Your Majesty, I will certainly use that," said the senator.

Upon returning to the U.S., the senator called in his chief-of-staff and asked, "Your mother has a child, and your father has a child, and this child is not your brother or your sister. Who is it?"

The chief-of-staff hemmed and hawed and finally asked, "Can I think about it and get back to you?"

The senator agreed and the chief-of-staff immediately called the smartest person he knew—his wife—and posed the question.

His wife answered immediately, "Why, it's me, of course."

Much relieved, the chief-of-staff rushed back to the senator and exclaimed, "I figured it out! It's my wife!"

The senator grimaced and replied in disgust, "Wrong, you idiot! It's the prime minister of England!"

"TO KNOW THAT YOU DO NOT KNOW IS THE BEST. TO PRETEND TO KNOW WHEN YOU DO NOT KNOW IS A DISEASE." LAO TZU

PROGRESS

23
Aim to Make Each Advance Count

Listening fills in the map of your situation, and aim studies that map to discover the best opportunity for changing your position.

Strategy uses **aim** to filter out what not to do so you focus.

Aim targets a *specific* way to advance your position by filtering out unnecessary activities.

Aim gives you focus. Picking the best opportunity to improve your position is essential for your success. Aim provides a system for picking the best openings that allow you to improve your position.

THE KEY TO AIMING: **You must clearly decide what to do and what not to do.**

Vision Comes From Aim

Vision is the ability to see a better future where others see only problems. Minimally, vision is the ability to see yourself playing a larger, more important role in the world. Vision is too big an idea for everyday strategy, but vision starts with simple aim. Over time, applying the simple skill of aim makes you look like a visionary.

Aim does makes you look like a visionary because it takes you away from the crowd. Opportunity is never what everyone thinks it is. By the time everyone sees something as an opportunity, it is no longer an opportunity.

Learning to Aim From Scratch

Aiming is not as difficult as listening, simply because there are fewer bad habits to break. Picking the right targets is a skill that most people need to learn from scratch.

Defend or Advance

The first purpose of aim is to determine whether you should defend your existing position or advance it. In some situations you can only defend. In others, you must advance.

Minimizing Risk in Advancing

In choosing among potential opportunities to advance, you have to consider what happens if you miss. Aim teaches a specific system of comparing the costs of advances in order to pick those with the fewest long-term risks.

A Path to the Future

If you succeed in advancing, what happens next? You must avoid putting yourself in a "better position" that makes future advances much more difficult.

"IT IS A PARADOXICAL BUT PROFOUNDLY TRUE AND IMPORTANT PRINCIPLE OF LIFE THAT THE MOST LIKELY WAY TO REACH A GOAL IS TO BE AIMING NOT AT THAT GOAL ITSELF BUT AT SOME MORE AMBITIOUS GOAL BEYOND IT." ARNOLD TOYNBEE

Opportunities are easy to pick when you have a strategic system for searching.

PROGRESS

24
Move It or Lose It

If aim is like picking out a destination on a map, then moving is the job of driving to that destination. Knowing where to go is one thing. Knowing how to get there is quite another. You need to act to change your position. A move can be a small action or a slight change in habit.

Strategy shows you how to complete **moves** to win new positions.

THE KEY TO MOVING: **You must take your commitments to completion.**

Adapting to the Situation

Getting from one position to another requires judgment. You have to pick the right path to get to your destination safely. Most people on the highway are just an accident waiting to happen. You must proceed at your own risk.

Get to the Opportunity on Time

When you move to an opportunity, you are like a driver trying to get to an appointment on time. The window of opportunity is closing. In order to make successful moves, you must master the three keys to getting to your opportunities quickly.

It Would Be Easy Except for Other People

Have you noticed that if you use your turn signal to let other drivers know that you are changing lanes, a lot of drivers will speed up to cut you off? Another principle of strategy—resistance—teaches that people will cut you off if they know where you are going. To manage the skill of moving, you must learn how not to signal your intentions in a way that creates opposition.

Traffic Conditions

You run into many different types of conditions on the road as you try to advance. You must recognize scattering conditions, easy conditions, disputed conditions, open conditions, shared conditions, bad conditions, dangerous conditions, tight conditions, and desperate conditions. Before you can know how to respond, you must know how to diagnose these conditions instantly.

The Nine Maneuvers

For each of these nine conditions, you need a maneuver to make the best progress. You must know the right maneuver to use and how to properly execute it. These maneuvers include diversion, taking, blocking, shadowing, alliance, perseverance, scrounging, surprise, and battle. Each one requires its own set of skills.

While strategy trains us to overcome our inborn instincts of flight or fight, it creates a new set of more productive instincts that reflexively find the best path forward.

Strategy teaches that nine situations require nine different maneuvers.

"LIFE IS AN ESCALATOR: YOU CAN MOVE FORWARD OR BACKWARD; YOU CAN NOT REMAIN STILL." PATRICIA RUSSELL-MCCLOUD

PROGRESS

25
Claim Without Shame

Success means making your advance pay off. This requires the final step of claiming your position to get a reward. If you win a car race, someone automatically gives you your prize. In real life, nothing is automatic. Making a claim is necessary because:

Strategy says you must **claim** your position to get its rewards.

THE WORLD IS NOT FAIR!

The world is full of people who make valuable contributions but who get less than they deserve. The world doesn't automatically reward people for their accomplishments.

THE KEY TO CLAIMING: **You must show others your worth.**

People only value what they can see. If you don't know how to make a claim, you will get less from your position than you could. You will not get the true value out of the advances you make, nor will you be able to defend your advances.

No one pays you for buying the winning lottery ticket unless you cash the it in. The people who get recognized are those who know what they have that others value. Every day, people throw away winning lottery tickets because their owners didn't know what they had.

Claiming requires:

- Knowing the relative value of positions
- Communication skills
- The courage to stand up for yourself

Making a Claim

Until you reach the claim step, you are a gold prospector. You listen to others' ideas about where the gold might be. You then sort through what you hear to choose the best place to look. You then move into that area and do the hard work of finding the gold.

However, when you find the gold, you must still know how to make your claim.

First, you have to prove your claim, that is, you have to find out if it is really worth working and owning.

Then, you must stake the limits of the claim, that is, you must identify what and how much ground you can realistically work.

Then, you must register your claim with others. You must tell other people about the ground you claim to protect your position.

Finally, you work the claim, getting the gold out of it one way or another.

Strategy is a system of getting recognition from others.

> "THE WORDS 'I AM...' ARE POTENT WORDS; BE CAREFUL WHAT YOU HITCH THEM TO. THE THING YOU'RE CLAIMING HAS A WAY OF REACHING BACK AND CLAIMING YOU." A. L. KITSELMAN

PROGRESS

26
THE KEYS TO PROGRESS

- Progress requires moving to strong positions, reacting to opposing moves, and using opportunities.
- The Progress Cycle requires repeating the steps of listening, aiming, moving, and claiming.
- The relationships on the Strategic Map define the elements of strategy more clearly than words alone.
- If you get stuck at any step in the Progress Cycle, you can break it down into smaller Progress Cycles.
- Making progress on your external position is more rewarding than internal progress.
- Dangers, distances, and obstacles must always be overcome to make progress.
- You must relearn how to LISTEN so that you don't filter out the opportunities that you hear.
- Picking the right opportunities using AIM requires a set of skills with which almost everyone is unfamiliar.
- Your ability to MOVE depends on recognizing nine situations and picking the appropriate responses.
- You get what you CLAIM, not what you deserve.

Part III
Listen to Discover Opportunities

I DON'T WORRY ABOUT GOING DEAF BECAUSE I STOPPED LISTENING WHEN I WAS A TEENAGER.

LISTEN

27 Stop Listening to the Mass Media

Why does strategy require you to listen to real live people? Can't you find opportunities by reading books and newspapers? Aren't there lots of opportunities to be found on the Internet? Does listening to television and the radio count as strategic listening?

The short answer is no, no, and, uh, NO!

Strategists avoid getting sucked in by the media.

Advancing your position means changing your relationship with people. It is the perceptions in people's minds that fuel every strategy because that is the information that defines your position. You cannot put media information into strategy and expect it to work.

Don't get me wrong. Reading is great. Television and radio are terrific. The Internet is an invaluable tool, making all manner of things easy that were once extremely difficult. I use the Internet daily for research.

Media information does not fit the needs of strategy. Strategy requires information with a special type of relevance.

Media Versus Real Human Contact

- Media information is too generic, too common.
- Media focuses on the past.
- Everyone has equal access to the media.

Real People Define the Real You

- Only people around you know your situation.
- Only people can tell you their intentions.
- Only people offer exclusive relationships.

You need information about your unique position. Only the people around you can know it. Opportunities arise only in the future. Only people know what they are planning for the future. There is no advantage in knowing what everyone knows and acting like everyone else acts. Strategy requires special knowledge, unknown to most, that allows you to move away from the crowd.

Get Brains Working for You

THE KEY OF ASKING: **Your questions can get other people's minds working for you.**

The point of listening is to use the power of as many human brains as possible. Asking questions gathers information, builds relationships, and triggers dialogue. Often you don't know the right questions. Only other people can guide you to asking them.

Strategy depends on regular contact with real people.

"LISTEN. DO NOT HAVE AN OPINION WHILE YOU LISTEN BECAUSE FRANKLY, YOUR OPINION DOESN'T HOLD MUCH WATER OUTSIDE OF YOUR UNIVERSE. JUST LISTEN. LISTEN UNTIL THEIR BRAIN HAS BEEN TWISTED LIKE A DRIPPING TOWEL AND WHAT THEY HAVE TO SAY IS ALL OVER THE FLOOR." HUGH ELLIOTT

28
Play Games With the Mad Monkey

Listening is the first step in the Progress Cycle and is a way of life. Strategy requires endless curiosity. The more you learn about your situation, the more easily you can advance it. The only way to learn about your situation is to listen to the people around you.

LISTEN

Unfortunately, as we approach our teen years, something happens to our ability to listen. We suddenly discern the folly of our parents' generation and realize that adults have nothing more to teach us. We then replace our minor listening skills with more entertaining talents, such as making smart remarks in response to any statement aimed at educating us.

As a friend explained when our own daughter was a teenager, "The teenage years are a gift given to parents so that they don't miss their children when they move out."

THE KEY OF SELECTIVE HEARING: **People only hear what they want to hear.**

Our minds are like mad monkeys. Without our conscious control, our minds:

- Pay minimum attention to what is said
- Spend free time planning future statements
- Find a lot of entertainment value in criticizing others

The Triple-Thick Barrier

When our thoughts and mouths take a break to focus on what other people are saying, we still block out most of what we hear. Over the years, we develop a wall of preconceptions, expectations, and assumptions. This triple-thick barrier is an effective prophylactic against opportunity.

Between thinking, talking, and filtering, we cannot hear the opportunities tapping so gently at our door.

Strategy teaches you how to open your mind to other points of view.

Making Listening Fun Again

Strategy addresses listening not by taming the mad monkey within, but by giving it bright, shiny toys with which to play. These toys put the fun back into listening and turn spotting opportunities into a series of games. Once you start playing these little games, you will be amazed at the interesting information you can acquire.

Strategic skills poke a few very special holes in the walls of your assumptions. We engineer these holes so that they are just the right size and shape to let in information about opportunities while still filtering out all that boring blather the world subjects us to.

> "WHEN I WAS A BOY OF FOURTEEN, MY FATHER WAS SO IGNORANT I COULD HARDLY STAND TO HAVE THE OLD MAN AROUND. BUT WHEN I GOT TO BE TWENTY-ONE, I WAS ASTONISHED AT HOW MUCH THE OLD MAN HAD LEARNED IN SEVEN YEARS." MARK TWAIN

29
THE "FIND THE OUTSIDER" GAME

Most people spend their time listening to people who share their perspective. Narrow listening results in narrow, limited viewpoints. Narrow, limited viewpoints create narrow, limited lives. If everything you hear only confirms what you already know, life is an echo, echo, echo chamber.

LISTEN

The Purpose of the Game

The purpose of playing "Find the Outsider" is to get different viewpoints on your situation. The more different ideas and different perspectives you get, the more broadly you see the world.

"Find the Outsider" is a simple game. You just keep track of the number of outsiders you listen to in a day, week, or month. Not how many outsiders you talk to, but how many outsiders you listen to, asking them for their perspective on your situation.

In this game, only outsiders count. Outsiders are people who are outside of your circle but close enough to see your situation. They don't have to know you personally, but they see some aspect—mission, climate, ground, command, or systems—of your position.

Who Is an Outsider?

Outsiders are a big, diverse group. Outsiders can be far above you, or below you, or just off in the distance somewhere. Outsiders include the janitor in your building, your boss's boss, a waitress at a local coffee shop, a next-door neighbor, a customer with whom your company does business, or the black sheep of the family.

A big group of outsiders are those you avoid because you don't agree with them. Truly courageous listeners seek out their opponents and rivals, not to fight with them but to listen to them.

Strategy teaches you to reach across boundaries for new ideas.

Perspective

All outsiders have something that you want and need. They have an outside perspective. They can see your strategic situation from angles you cannot even imagine.

Perspective is a simple idea. Everything close to you appears big. Everything more distant appears smaller. From a limited perspective, you cannot see your true position, especially its relationship with the other positions around you.

- Good or bad things lurk hidden around the corner.
- Outside views see the world from different angles.
- New angles reveal what is hidden from your viewpoint.

Just by listening to outsiders, you will broaden your circle of contacts. One outsider can lead you to another. If you talk to one outsider a day, you will hear about more opportunities than you can imagine.

> "A GOOD LISTENER IS NOT ONLY POPULAR EVERYWHERE, BUT AFTER A WHILE HE GETS TO KNOW SOMETHING." WILSON MIZNER

LISTEN

30 The "Who's Fooling Whom" Game

There is an old saying in poker, "If you don't know who the sucker is at the table, you are the sucker." You don't want to be paranoid when you are listening, but suspicion is a valuable tool.

Strategists learn to suspect deception everywhere.

LISTEN

- Some people deceive others.
- Others delude themselves.
- Many think they are deceiving but are only deluding themselves.

Listening is a challenge in a world so full of deception and delusion.

Deception in the form of bluffing is extremely useful in strategy, but deluding yourself about your situation is the worst of strategic sins.

One Person's Truth

A simple game helps you test the quality of the information that you are hearing. The game has four simple steps.

1. Delay making judgments. Avoid judging statements as true or false when you first hear them, especially when they are from a new source. It takes time to tell whether or not people are deceiving you.

2. Spot the difference between words and actions. Words are cheap. Actions have costs. Actions can be used to mislead, but when you see a difference between words and actions, trust the actions.

3. Filter words through mission and command. The more you

know about people's goals and character, the better you can guess what they want you to believe and why.

4. Find the patterns. Listening collects pieces of a puzzle *and* puts them together. If a piece doesn't fit the pattern, you flip it around and then see if it fits.

Notice that these steps cannot tell you whether any deception is intentional or the result of self-delusion.

How You Lose the Game

If you let someone know that you suspect that they are trying to fool you, you instantly lose the game. When playing this game, you NEVER point out the inconsistencies you discover.

How You Win the Game

You win when you can use deception to discover the truth. After awhile, "Who's Fooling Whom" creates a reality readjustment lens. This lens automatically reshapes what each person tells you, bending their deceptions back into a close approximation of the truth. At the poker table, you learn who bets aggressively and who bets timidly. You can use this information to gauge the real contents of their hand against your own.

Strategy teaches you how to interpret everything you hear.

"IN GENERAL, THE GREATER THE UNDERSTANDING, THE GREATER THE DELUSION: THE MORE INTELLIGENT, THE LESS SANE." GEORGE ORWELL

31 THE "EVERYTHING IS BACKWARDS" GAME

LISTEN

In strategy, everything works the opposite of what you expect. This makes strategy counterintuitive. You have to develop a skill for turning every coin over to see what is on the other side.

People say opposites attract. Strategy says:

- ☯ Environments and competitors are joined opposites.
- ( ) Conditions create their opposites.

It then takes this idea one crazy step further.

> THE KEY OF REVERSAL: **Every condition gives rise over time to its opposite condition.**

The point of thinking backwards is to spot opportunities before they arise. Through the alchemy of competition, slow organizations create faster competitors. Large organizations generate smaller competitors. Problems create opportunities.

The Rules of the Game

You can stimulate your backwards thinking with the "Everything Is Backwards" game.

1. Notice whenever anyone uses a descriptive adjective.

2. When they do, ask yourself, "Compared to what?" Is the comparison with other objects or with the larger environment itself?

3. Ask yourself, "What is this condition's opposite?"

4. Ask yourself, "How will this condition create its opposite?"

5. Ask yourself, "How can I use this coming change?

The Theory of Relativity

What is "good"? What is "bad"? What is "fast"? What is "slow"? These descriptive adjectives take their meaning from comparisons. An alternative is neither good nor bad in itself. It is only good or bad when compared with other alternatives. You have to know what people mean when they describe things. Often, they don't know what they mean themselves.

People can compare apples with apples. They can compare apples with oranges. They can also compare apples to the tree they are growing on. Consider a big fish in a little pond. A fish that looks big in a pond looks small in a lake. The context of the environment determines our perceptions about the qualities of things in the environment, and strategy requires using those perceptions.

Reversing the context is the source of both opportunity and jokes. Consider the fortune-teller who read a woman's palm.

"There's no easy way to say this," said the psychic sadly. "But you must prepare yourself for becoming a widow. Your husband will die a violent and painful death within a few months."

Visibly shaken, the woman felt tears well up in her eyes. After taking few deep breaths, she asked in a quavering voice:

"Will I be convicted?"

Strategists find opportunities by looking at things upside-down.

"THE OPPOSITE OF A CORRECT STATEMENT IS A FALSE STATEMENT. BUT THE OPPOSITE OF A PROFOUND TRUTH MAY WELL BE ANOTHER PROFOUND TRUTH."
NIELS BOHR

32
THE "MAGICAL TWIST" GAME

Like a good mystery story, the science of strategy has a twist.

THE KEY OF SIMPLIFICATION: **All strategic conditions are reduced to either "empty" or "full."**

LISTEN

Strategy Is Simple

Emptiness is need. Fullness is what satisfies that need. Happiness, bigness, satiation, speed, and knowledge are forms of fullness. Sadness, smallness, hunger, slowness, and ignorance are types of emptiness. Happiness satisfies sadness. Satisfaction fulfills hunger. Knowledge fills up ignorance, and so on.

How can you know if a condition has strategic importance? When you listen, it's too complicated to keep track of every possible condition. So you listen for forms of the two most basic conditions.

The Magical Twist

Three related concepts come together like this:

- ☯ Completeness comes from opposites.
- () Strategic conditions create their opposites.
- ⌛ All conditions can be reduced to empty or full.

The next step is what works strategy's magic:

THE KEY OF INVERSION: **ANY empty condition can create ANY full condition and vice versa.**

Conditions not only create their exact opposites—for example, small creating large—but any empty condition can create any full condition or any full condition some type of emptiness. This means that small can create fast, ignorance can create large, focus can create small, and so on. This sounds crazy, but small forces move more quickly than large ones. Ignorance imagines large opponents. Focus aims at small targets. Inversion opens your mind to many unexpected conditions that can create opportunities.

LISTEN

The Rules of the "Magical Twist" Game

1. When you hear about a condition, you ask yourself, "Does that situation describe an empty state?"

2. If the condition is a form of emptiness, you continue the game by asking, "What form of fullness can this weakness create?"

3. You win the game if you can answer the final question: "Is there a way that I can fill this empty state to put myself in a position of greater strength?"

Strategy looks for trends to reverse themselves.

An opportunity is an empty, needy condition that you can use to advance your position. By using the magical twist, you imagine how conditions might create new forms of emptiness in the future. Listening is part of this game. You empty yourself, listening now to think later. Only by becoming empty can you fill yourself with knowledge.

"STRENGTH IS JUST AN ACCIDENT ARISING FROM THE WEAKNESS OF OTHERS." JOSEPH CONRAD

33
The "Looking for Trouble" Game

Strategy teaches that there will always be an infinite amount of opportunity because opportunity comes from emptiness and need. People always have needs. It is human nature. No matter what your specific situation, every person that you come in contact with has needs. Through the magical twist of emptiness and fullness, you can always translate these needs into opportunities.

LISTEN

Unfortunately, people are conditioned to:

- See needs as problems rather than opportunities
- Have their needs blind them to the needs of others
- Ignore and forget the problems they learn about

Rules for the "Looking for Trouble" Game

In this game, you focus on listening uncritically to other people's problems.

1. Ask people about the problems and needs that they have.
2. Ask people about others who have needs and problems.
3. Gather information about the needs that create problems.

This game trains you to do the opposite of what people more commonly do. Most people don't want to hear about anyone else's problems. Most people can politely offer sympathy or even advice, but it is much easier to criticize the needs of others than to understand them. You must train yourself in listening to get a broad sampling of the types of problems the people you deal with encounter.

Consider the problems of a lawyer who opened the door of his BMW on a busy street when suddenly a car came along and hit the door, ripping it off completely. When the police arrived at the scene, the lawyer was complaining bitterly about the damage to his precious BMW.

"Officer, look what they've done to my Beeeeemer!" he whined.

"You lawyers are so materialistic—you make me sick!" retorted the officer. "You're so worried about your stupid BMW, that you didn't even notice that your left arm was ripped off!"

"Oh, my gaaawd," cried the lawyer, finally noticing the bloody left shoulder where his arm used to be. "Where's my Rolex?!"

As this story illustrates, our perceptions of problems are not always the same as other people's. The purpose of the "Looking for Trouble Game" is to develop your acceptance and understanding of other people's views of the situation. There are no right or wrong needs. There is only a broader perspective.

Since an opening is an emptiness that you can fill, your opportunities—when they come—will come from seeking out these problems. Problems and opportunities are two sides of the same coin.

Strategy finds opportunities in problems.

"OPPORTUNITY IS MISSED BY MOST PEOPLE BECAUSE IT IS DRESSED IN OVERALLS AND LOOKS LIKE WORK." THOMAS A. EDISON

LISTEN

34
That Hollow Empty Feeling

Opportunity and emptiness are closely connected through the idea of an opening.

> THE KEY TO OPENINGS: **Opportunities are an emptiness that you can get rewarded for filling.**

You cannot push people to create openings. Opportunities are gifts that other people—often your opponents and rivals—give you.

There is a story about two young couples, the Wilsons and the Smiths. They were friends who grew up together in the same small town and moved to the same big city, but they were also rivals.

Both couples were short on cash and traveling by train back to their high school class reunion. At the station, Mr. and Mrs. Wilson each bought a ticket, but they were surprised to see that the Smiths purchased only one ticket.

"How are the two of you going to travel on only one ticket?" asked Mrs. Wilson.

"Watch and learn," answered Mrs. Smith with a superior wink.

The Wilsons took their seats on the train but the Smiths both crammed into the toilet together and closed the door. After the train departed the station, the conductor came through the car collecting tickets. He knocked on the toilet door and said, "Ticket, please."

The door opened a crack and a woman's arm emerged with a ticket in hand. The conductor took it and moved on. The Wilsons saw how this worked and agreed that it was an interesting idea.

On the return trip, the Smiths again bought a single ticket, but the Wilsons didn't buy any ticket at all.

"How can you travel without any ticket?" asked Mrs. Smith.

"Watch and learn," answered Mrs. Wilson with a superior wink.

On the train, the Wilsons crammed themselves into one toilet while the Smiths crammed themselves into another toilet.

Just after the train left the station, Mrs. Wilson sent her husband up to the car with the Smiths' toilet. He knocked on their door and said, "Ticket, please."

Gifts From Rivals

When your opponents forget to defend themselves well, it creates a problem for them and an opening for you. Again, your actions are judged in comparison with those of others. The most effective actions are those that take advantage of the weakness of rivals, strengthening your position at the expense of theirs.

Strategists listen to opponents to discover openings.

"WHEN MEN ARE BROUGHT FACE TO FACE WITH THEIR OPPONENTS, FORCED TO LISTEN AND LEARN AND MEND THEIR IDEAS, THEY CEASE TO BE CHILDREN AND SAVAGES AND BEGIN TO LIVE LIKE CIVILIZED MEN." WALTER LIPPMANN

35
IT TAKES ALL KINDS OF PEOPLE

No discussion of listening would be complete without covering what types of people you need to seek out and when. The word "networking" suggests a haphazard approach to building information channels. Strategy teaches a more focused approach.

A Range of Contacts

Knowing a lot of people is not the same as having a well-developed circle of contacts. Strategy teaches that the number of contacts matters less than the range and quality of your contacts. You need people from several different categories to complete a circle of contacts. The question is: how do you categorize people?

Egotists divide people into three groups: those who are like them, those who want to be like them, and those who have no ambition.

Government economists also divide people into three groups: those who can count and those who can't.

Bookmakers, on the other hand, divide people into those who make things happen, those who watch things happen, and those who wonder what happened.

Strategy divides contacts into five groups:

- **Leaders** articulate a mission.
- **Guides** know the ground.

- **Hot-spotters** are close to a change.
- **Insiders** are close to decision-makers.
- **Operators** understand particular systems.

A Well-Rounded Group

The best people to listen to are leaders whose example you can emulate. If you meet a hundred successful people, you will find that they all have highly developed information channels and highly developed skills at collecting and managing their personal contacts. This is especially true of people who repeat their success. The biography of anyone who has repeated success demonstrates the critical role that past contacts played in their future success.

Guides are people with experience on a particular competitive ground. Seek guides when you move into new areas.

Strategy requires a well-rounded group of contacts.

Hot-spotters are people who are close to changes in your competitive arena. You seek these people when you first hear about a change, but, ideally, they will seek you out.

Insiders are those who can give you insight into the character of a decision-maker whose decisions affect you. Seek insiders when you first learn that a certain person is important to your future.

Operators are people who know how a particular type of system works. Seek operators when you need to learn new systems.

> "ISN'T IT INTERESTING THAT THE SAME PEOPLE WHO LAUGH AT SCIENCE FICTION LISTEN TO WEATHER FORECASTS AND ECONOMISTS?" KELVIN THROOP III

36
The Leader of the Pack

Leaders serve as examples to emulate, but strategy teaches that following alone is dangerous. Our normal instincts are exactly wrong when it comes to listening to leaders. Cows, lemmings, and people are herd animals. We like the comfort of being part of a crowd. Even when leaders behave foolishly, we keep following. You cannot be successful as a blind follower.

Loners, Followers, and Leaders

Strategy is a discipline for assuming control of your life. No true loner is ever successful, because we all need other people. All leaders start as followers, learning the art from good examples. There is a tremendous difference, however, between people who follow to learn to lead and those who follow to avoid deciding for themselves.

Many so-called leaders can teach you nothing about leadership. I am reminded of a foreign visitor who stood outside the U.S. Congress without knowing what it was.

He asked the guard, "How do I get to work there?"

"What are you, an idiot?" responded the guard.

"Is that required?" asked the visitor.

Great leaders take you away from the crowd. A crowded territory is a form of fullness. Moving toward fullness creates weakness. Leaders take you into new areas to discover opportunities.

Strategists Are Pioneers

Leaders teach you how to explore new territories. Being a pioneer requires all five characteristics of command. Leaders must:

- Care about others' needs
- Be smart to learn new ground
- Have courage to face change
- Be disciplined to avoid crowds
- Win the trust of followers

Strategy dares to go where no one has gone before.

Leaders realize that success means filling emptiness. An opening of emptiness makes an opportunity possible, but leadership is required to recognize and use opportunities.

To use strategy, you have to make decisions for yourself. We are all leaders in our private lives. You can learn from leaders in your public life, but at some point you must become an explorer, a pioneer on your own.

The Pride of Followers

You can rely on the inertia of herd instinct. People take pride in thinking that others are sheep. To secularists, the religious are sheep. To the religious, secularists are sheep. To people in one political party, people in the other party are sheep. All this means is that most prefer their own crowd to the other guy's crowd.

> "IT IS VERY EASY IN THE WORLD TO LIVE BY THE OPINION OF THE WORLD. IT IS VERY EASY IN SOLITUDE TO BE SELF-CENTERED. BUT THE FINISHED MAN IS HE WHO IN THE MIDST OF THE CROWD KEEPS WITH PERFECT SWEETNESS THE INDEPENDENCE OF SOLITUDE." RALPH WALDO EMERSON

LISTEN

37 GOING COMPLETELY NATIVE

Since strategy means you are always advancing your position, your progress continually takes you into new fertile ground for exploration. As you move into these new areas, you need to make contact with the local natives who can be your guides, teaching you the lay of the land and the local customs.

New ground is defined as any situation with which you are unfamiliar. When you are hired by a new employer, you need to make friends with longtime employees. When your child goes to a new school, you need to make contact with other parents at that school. In romantic matters, you need to make contact with people who are more experienced than you are.

An Army Ranger deployed overseas received a "Dear John" letter from his girlfriend. She told him that she had slept with other guys while he had been gone, wanted to break up, and wanted the pictures he had of her sent back.

The young soldier didn't know how to respond so he went to his sergeant. The sergeant went around to the camp and collected all the unwanted photos of women that he could find.

The sergeant had the soldier mail several dozen pictures to his girlfriend with the following note:

"I'm sorry but I can't remember which one you are, but please take the one that belongs to you and send the rest back. Thank you."

Admitting Ignorance Creates Strength

Strategists accept the keys that others offer them.

Our herd instinct and ego combine to make seeking out guides harder than it should be.

When you are new to an area, you are naturally more comfortable with other people who are also new. People like us make up our natural herd. The problem is that those people cannot help you.

Most people would rather hide their lack of experience than emphasize it. Again, people come in three types, those who know, those who don't know, and those who pretend to know.

Fill Emptiness or Others Will

If you fill your emptiness, you create strength. If you let others use your emptiness as an opening, they create strength for themselves. While you want to keep your weaknesses a secret, you have to admit your limitations and ask for help before you can develop strength. The faster you can get access to people with this expertise, the fewer mistakes you will make and the faster you will advance in the future.

"IT IS THE PROVINCE OF KNOWLEDGE TO SPEAK AND IT IS THE PRIVILEGE OF WISDOM TO LISTEN." OLIVER WENDELL HOLMES

38
GET IT WHILE IT'S HOT

In today's dynamic environment, things change quickly. Most changes that will affect your life do not show up on the nightly news. A relative takes ill. Your company is acquired. You cannot control the changing climate, so you need information quickly.

Who knows about those changes? Again, you can find out about what is happening right now only from people who are in touch with what is happening now. The faster you can learn about decisions that affect you, the better positioned you are to deal with those changes.

Strategy teaches how to get information quickly.

Create an Early Warning System

You need to develop relationships with people in potential "hot spots" in your life. You need to work to develop contacts inside every group with which you have dealings. You create an "early warning system" of contacts in every area where changes can take place. These people need not be decision-makers, but regular people who are positioned in the right place to get information early.

In your career, you can develop relationships with people who have contact with your rivals or competitors. If bureaucratic decisions can affect you, you need to know people in those government offices. This includes people at your children's schools. In potential romantic relationships, you need contact with your beloved's friends and relatives who are willing to keep you informed.

Take Advantage of Opportunities

When stuff happens, even bad stuff, the event is an opportunity to develop a contact. When you develop contacts, let them know that you would appreciate it if they would:

- Keep you informed about events in the future
- Give you a heads-up **before** such events happen

Looking to the Future

People create the future by acting on their plans today. The sooner we learn about plans, the more options we have in acting on that information. Given the right information, we can even prevent things from happening that we want to avoid.

A woman in New York had parents who retired to Phoenix. On a visit, the woman met her parents' next-door neighbor and secretly asked her to call if the parents ever had a problem. One day she got a call from that neighbor.

"I hate to ruin your day," the neighbor said. "But I wanted to warn you that your parents are getting a divorce."

"What are you talking about?" asked the woman.

"Your mother told me she already has an attorney," the neighbor explained. "And your father is packing to move to an apartment."

The woman immediately called Phoenix and screamed at her mother: "You are NOT getting divorced! Don't do a single thing until I get there. Our whole family will be out tomorrow. Until then, don't do a thing. DO YOU HEAR ME?" And she hung up.

The mother immediately called her neighbor and said, "Just wanted to thank you. My daughter and her family are coming for Christmas and paying their own way."

39
Low People in High Places

The command of people over you means people's decisions can affect your strategic position. You should develop relationships with these people when possible, but you cannot always get close to these decision-makers themselves. It is especially difficult to get in close with people whose decisions affect a lot of people.

Lots of Possibilities

Powerful decision-makers come in regular contact with secretaries, gardeners, grocers, dentists, in-laws, and other disinterested parties who can provide valuable information. These people cannot give you insight into planning, but they can give you insight into an individual's character. It can be surprising how much they know.

A small-town district attorney called a grandmotherly, elderly woman as a witness. He approached her and asked, "Mrs. Wilson, do you know me?"

She said, "Certainly, I do know you, Mr. Smith. I've known you since you were a young boy. And frankly, you've been a big disappointment to me. You lie, you cheat on your wife, you manipulate people and talk about them behind their backs. You think you're a rising big shot when you haven't the brains to realize you never will amount to anything more than a two-bit paper pusher. Yes, I know you."

The DA was stunned. Not knowing what else to do, he pointed

across the room and asked, "Mrs. Wilson, do you know the defense attorney?"

She again replied, "Why, yes I do. I used to baby-sit him for his parents. And he, too, has been a real disappointment to me. He's lazy, bigoted, and he has a drinking problem. The man can't maintain a normal relationship with anyone and his law practice is one of the most crooked in the entire state. Yes, I know him."

At this point the judge rapped the courtroom to silence and called both lawyers to the bench. In a very quiet voice, he threatened, "You are dangerously close to contempt of court. If either of you asks her if she knows me, you're going to jail."

Making Friends

These insiders may be shy about providing information unless you make them your friends. You can often reward these contacts simply by paying attention to them, especially service people who are so often ignored by the powerful.

"THERE WAS A DEFINITE PROCESS BY WHICH ONE MADE PEOPLE INTO FRIENDS, AND IT INVOLVED TALKING TO THEM AND LISTENING TO THEM FOR HOURS AT A TIME." REBECCA WEST

40 Smooth Operators

Only fools try to invent all the systems that they need for themselves. You wouldn't be reading this book unless you were interested in developing new skills in the system of strategy. The best way to learn new skills is to develop relationships with people who already know those systems.

Operators Are Better Than Experts

You want to seek out and listen to people who use a system, not necessarily the "experts" in those systems. Experts are usually more invested in telling what you cannot do rather than what you can do. Operators know what is really possible because they are doing it.

For example, you may know someone who is good at developing and maintaining a circle of contacts. Rather than reading in more detail about systems for networking, you should make contact with that person and start listening to what he or she does.

Of course, there are many systems you can learn directly from people. Generally, it is best to learn from someone who practices a skill effectively rather than someone who just teaches that skill. Practical knowledge is a matter of knowing how all the parts work together. People who understand the machinery of systems can get a lot of work done with very little actual work.

Consider the 85-year-old man who lived alone in the country and needed to plant a garden but couldn't till the soil. His only son used to help him, but he was in prison for insider trading. The old man wrote a letter describing his problem.

"Dear Son: It looks like I won't be able to plant my garden this year. I'm just getting too old to dig up that hard ground. If you were just here, I know you would help me. Love, Papa"

A few days later, the old man received a letter back from his son.

"Dear Papa: Don't dig up that garden. That's where I buried all my money & stock certificates. Your Loving Son"

Early the next morning, FBI agents and local police showed up in the garden with a backhoe and dug up the entire area. When they didn't find any money or stocks, they apologized to the old man and left. The following day the old man received another letter.

"Dear Papa: You can plant your garden now. It's the best I could do under the circumstances. Love, Your Son"

"PRACTICAL WISDOM IS ONLY TO BE LEARNED IN THE SCHOOL OF EXPERIENCE. PRECEPTS AND INSTRUCTION ARE USEFUL SO FAR AS THEY GO, BUT, WITHOUT THE DISCIPLINE OF REAL LIFE, THEY REMAIN OF THE NATURE OF THEORY ONLY." SAMUEL SMILES

Strategy relies on every person's natural desire to pass on what he or she has learned to others.

LISTEN

41
Keeping Everyone Happy, Happy

Strategic information is not free. It depends on relationships. Some of these relationships are like marriages. They cost a great deal of time, effort, and money. Though information can be expensive, the broad access to information is worth more than anything else in strategy. You must prize it and prize the way that it advances your position. Developing and maintaining a contact network requires time every day.

Strategy would be easy if it weren't for all the people involved.

Return the Favor

An important way you reward your contacts is by giving them information that they might find valuable. If you have a well-developed contact network, much of the information that comes your way won't be relevant to your situation, but it will be relevant to someone else in your circle. If you take the time to pass that information on, it will buy you a similar return favor in the future.

One smart couple puts together a list of contacts for services in their neighborhood. When a new neighbor moves in, this couple brings their list with a welcome basket. The list includes recommendations for local plumbers, gardeners, home repair, car service, restaurants, stores, and so on.

The new neighbors are encouraged to introduce themselves to these service providers, telling them who recommended them. This not only helps the new people by giving them a circle of contacts, but wins this smart couple great service from all these establishments on their list.

Keep Relationships Special

People value being an insider. They like feeling part of an elite group. You must treat your contacts as if they are valuable. You can do this in three ways:

- Keep your relationships a secret.
- Clearly express your appreciation.
- Ask them to open your eyes.

Secrecy is always valuable in strategy, but even when it seems that no damage will be done by letting others know about a relationship, you should avoid broadcasting relationships unless it helps the contacts themselves.

You must express your appreciation both for the relationship and for the efforts that people make to keep you informed, regardless of the quality of information provided at any given contact.

You must also express your appreciation for viewpoints that differ from your own. The more different the viewpoint, the more clearly you must express your appreciation. You can never know what information will be the key to a valuable opportunity.

"WE WILL NEVER BE ABLE TO MAKE A MACHINE THAT WILL ASK QUESTIONS. THE ABILITY TO ASK THE RIGHT QUESTION IS MORE THAN HALF THE BATTLE OF FINDING THE ANSWER." THOMAS J. WATSON

42 The "Who Do You Trust?" Game

Strategically, it is always safer to listen than it is to talk.

> THE KEY OF SECRECY: **Your success depends upon keeping your own plans secret.**

LISTEN

Trading Secrets

Because of this principle, there is a strategic problem at the heart of all communication.

- Information channels depend on trading information.
- Everything you say can be used against you.

The best contacts are those who simply like having others listen to them. However, many critical relationships are built on trust, and trust is built by trading confidences. If you don't trust others with any sensitive information, few will trust you with the most valuable forms of information.

The more contacts you have, the more information you can get and the broader the potential exposure of your secrets. The world is competitive. If you give people the weapon of information, they will use it to their own ends.

Secrecy and Strategy

Strategy teaches flexible opportunism over rigid planning because long-term, fixed plans are easily discovered. The quicker your reactions, the fewer plans you have to share with others. What you share with others must be carefully measured and packaged for consumption. You cannot control information once you let it out. What your friends know, your enemies will soon know as well. Even those closest to you—your spouse, for example—will use stuff against you if you give him or her the wrong information in the wrong package at the wrong time.

Stategy uses secrets to build relationships while minimizing risks.

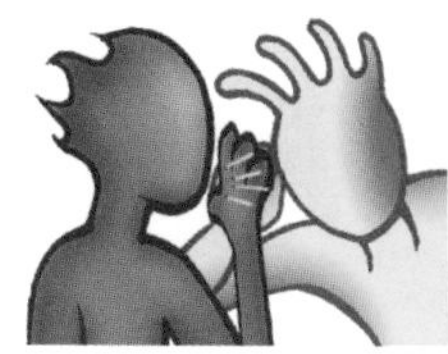

The Rules of the Game

You use the "Who Do You Trust" game to tie people to you in a deeper relationship.

1. Know where contacts stand before sharing any secret. Know their mission, their character, and the people with whom their systems put them into contact.

2. Consider how their position will change when you share information with them. This act changes the relationship. For example, if you tell your best friend that his spouse is cheating on him, you may well destroy your relationship rather than secure it.

3. Before you speak, you must have them agree to the rules protecting that information. These rules must be simple and easy to honor. If a friend is a police officer, don't expect him or her to keep confidences about criminal activity.

4. If your contacts share secrets in return, you must always keep their confidence. Nothing will uncover your secrets faster than revealing other people's secrets.

"DO NOT TRUST ALL MEN, BUT TRUST MEN OF WORTH; THE FORMER COURSE IS SILLY, THE LATTER A MARK OF PRUDENCE." DEMOCRITUS

43 The Secret of Mind Control

Secrecy is a constant preoccupation of strategy, bringing together the principles of deception, emptiness, fullness, and managing sources of information. For 2,500 years, people kept strategy secret because information about how it works gives you power.

LISTEN

Strategy teaches you how to control people's perceptions.

THE KEY TO CONTROL: **You move others by changing their perceptions.**

The Elusive Nature of "Truth"

Listening gives you information. You need information to understand your position and the positions of other people. People act on the information. If you understand their position, you should see the potential effect of specific information on their actions.

Ignorance is a form of emptiness. If you can control how that information gets filled, you can control how people act. You can easily push them toward the void created by their hopes and fears.

You gather information so that you can understand the situation well enough to control people with a minimum of effort. People keep secrets because they don't want to be controlled. People are easier to control because they know that they don't have all the information.

A fancy coiffured French poodle was lost by her owner on a safari in the jungles of Africa. Wandering about, the poodle noticed a leopard heading rapidly in her direction with the obvious intention of having lunch.

The poodle spied some bones on the ground nearby and immediately settled down to chew on them with her back to the approaching cat. Just as the leopard was about to leap, the poodle exclaimed loudly, "Boy, that was one delicious leopard. I wonder if there are any more around here."

The leopard halted his attack in mid-stride. He suddenly realized that he didn't know what type of creature this was. He crept carefully away, thinking, "Whew, that was close. That strange animal nearly had me."

Meanwhile, a monkey had been watching the scene from a nearby tree. He figured that he could put this information to good use and chased after the leopard. The poodle heard the monkey swinging after the leopard and wondered what was going on.

The monkey caught up with the leopard, offered a deal trading information for protection, and explained what the poodle had done. The leopard was furious. He told the monkey, "Climb on my back and we'll see how tough this fluffy animal really is."

The poodle had secretly followed the monkey and overheard them talking. When they started looking for her, she ran a distance away but then stopped in a clearing where they could easily find her. As the two animals approached, she sat with her back toward them. Just as they got close enough to hear her, the poodle said, "Where's that damn monkey? I sent him off half an hour ago to bring me another leopard! What could be taking so long?"

44
The Keys to Listening

- Research is fine, but opportunities can only be discovered by making contact with real people and listening.
- To recognize opportunities, you discard your assumptions and stop thinking and talking.
- People who have very different points of view from your own are more likely to help you see opportunities.
- Your opportunities come from emptiness, openings, and the needs of others.
- The herd instinct takes you away from opportunities; the pioneer spirit takes you toward them.
- You cannot create opportunities; you can only recognize them when they arise.
- You need to seek out guides, hot-spotters, insiders, and operators to help you identify opportunities.
- Information is the key to finding new opportunities, and you must be willing to invest in it.
- You must protect information about your own position while sharing information with others.

Part IV
Aim at a Specific Opportunity

45 The Path of Most Assistance

When you listen, you are wide open to possibilities. You listen to learn as much as you can. As you move to the next step, you reverse that process. You narrow your options to the best possible action. You can do only one thing at a time. At any given moment, you must decide how to spend your limited time.

> THE KEY OF EASE: **You must choose the best possible EASY task to do right now.**

The surprising word here is "easy." Strategy aims for openings. The idea is to make progress easy, not to burn yourself out or beat your head against a wall.

AIM

Envisioning a New Position

A new position must exist in the mind before it can be made real.

You aim with the end in mind. You need a clear sense of what you want your new position to be. Aim sees beyond the opening to where it leads. When you think about the position for which you are aiming, you must consider:

- Long-term goals
- Getting what you need
- Leveraging coming changes
- Suitability to your character
- Fit with your past skills

Everything and More

Most new positions are almost like your old position only a little different. The question is, how is the new position better?

Aim starts with your mission. Without long-term goals, you cannot pick a near-term target. This connection of short-term decisions to long-term goals is what separates strategic moves from merely tactical ones. Does the move take you in the right direction?

Aim also considers the environment. How will the move expand or change the ground you control to better support your mission? How are the trends of change supporting your movement to that ground and supporting the mission?

Aim is only about you. How does a move play into your personal strengths and weakness? What must you learn to do differently to secure the benefits of the advance?

Creating the Future

Vision not only foresees the future; it creates it. You play an active role in what is possible. No matter what your current position and what your goal, you always have options for improving your position. Each decision creates new possibilities.

> "THE FUTURE IS NOT A RESULT OF CHOICES AMONG ALTERNATIVE PATHS OFFERED BY THE PRESENT, BUT A PLACE THAT IS CREATED—CREATED FIRST IN THE MIND AND WILL, CREATED NEXT IN ACTIVITY. THE FUTURE IS NOT SOME PLACE WE ARE GOING TO, BUT ONE WE ARE CREATING. THE PATHS ARE NOT TO BE FOUND, BUT MADE, AND THE ACTIVITY OF MAKING THEM, CHANGES BOTH THE MAKER AND THE DESTINATION." JOHN SCHAAR

46
How to Develop a Narrow Mind

Aim means doing less, not more. People think that:

- Becoming successful requires doing more and more
- Those who do the most get the most done

Strategy teaches that this thinking is backwards in a bad way.

> The Key of Less Is More: **Doing less is always more successful than doing more.**

Aim is mostly a process of elimination. Doing the right thing is 90 percent avoiding the wrong thing. The reality is:

- ☑ Most effort goes into activities that are wasted.
- ☑ You can learn how to avoid wasting your efforts.

You cannot do everything. You have only so much time, energy, and effort in you. If you eliminate everything that you shouldn't do, you are left with more resources to apply to the things that are more valuable. Success requires:

- Eliminating everything that you don't have to do
- Doing only one thing at a time and doing it well
- Concentrating efforts over time on a few tasks

Without aim, the tendency is to pursue everything that looks like an opportunity as soon as it comes along.

AIM

A Commitment to Action

Aim is a commitment to action. It is the conscious choice of making one particular move to advance your position. You cannot go two different directions at once. When you choose a move, you must commit to finish it and not let yourself get distracted along the way.

After having three books on computers published by Bantam Books, I joined with two other Radio Shack veterans to start a software consulting business.

PCWEEK
Inside
Inside People: HIGH TECH FEASTS ON A FAST-FOOD DIET SEE PAGE A/4 FOR THE SECRET RECIPES FROM TWO NEW EXECS
FORWARD SPIN
Prices are higher; the market is wide open, and competition is scarce. So where's this Nirvana? It's Japan, gaijin.
Software Samurai
BY STEVE HAMM
SON OF SUN TZU

At first, we would do any type of computer work people wanted, but then we focused on database development, and our company grew.

After that, we did any type of database work, but then we narrowed our focus to accounting systems, and our company grew.

Then we sold accounting systems both to businesses directly and to resellers who installed our software. Then we focused just on selling to resellers alone, and our company grew.

At first we worked with any type of software reseller. Most worked with small companies, but a few worked with large companies. Then we focused on working with resellers who sold only to larger corporations, and our company grew.

At first, we worked with large companies through resellers, but a few large corporations wanted to work with us directly. We focused on working with these few companies, and our company grew.

The whole time, our software company did less and less. Eventually, we did so little that we became one of *Inc.* magazine's 500 fastest-growing companies in America.

47 The Extraordinary From the Ordinary

Opportunity comes in two flavors, the ordinary and the extraordinary. Most moves you make are ordinary, but ordinary moves are not enough to create real momentum in your life.

THE KEY TO MOMENTUM: **The expected must be combined with the unexpected.**

A series of successes does not create momentum if the successes are expected. Momentum is created when a surprise happens. However, as a complementary opposite, surprise isn't possible unless something else is expected. This means you must:

- Use standard methods to meet everyday challenges
- Use unexpected methods to win big breakthroughs

AIM

Standards and Breakthroughs

Most opportunities advance your position through standard, obvious activities. You advance relationships by spending time with people, sharing experiences, and helping them with their problems. You advance your career by doing your duties, learning about your company, and expanding your skills.

If you learn to use strategy consistently to make ordinary advances, you put yourself in position for an extraordinary breakthrough. Surprising breakthroughs arise when ordinary expected methods are changed in some way that seems obvious.

The Two Sources of Surprise

- Mix two common things to make something new.
- Bring common knowledge in one area to a new area.

The "electronic spreadsheet" is the first kind of surprise. Spreadsheets are hundreds of years old. Calculating software existed for dozens of years. Putting them together created something new and powerful.

The Golden Key to Strategy is the second type of breakthrough. Strategy has been used in war and in business for a long time, but this book is the first to take its principles and apply them to everyone every day.

Strategy is a source of endless invention and creativity.

There was once an aspiring veterinarian who put himself through veterinary school working nights as a taxidermist.

Upon graduation, he decided he could combine his two vocations to better serve the needs of his patients and their owners, while doubling his practice and, therefore, his income.

He opened his own offices with a shingle on the door saying, "Dr. Jones, Veterinary Medicine and Taxidermy —Either way, you get your dog back!"

"IT'S JUST THE WAY THAT THESE EXPERTS TEND TO TALK ABOUT STRATEGY—AS IF IT IS SOME KIND OF HIGH-BRAIN, SCIENTIFIC METHODOLOGY—FEELS REALLY OFF TO ME."
JACK WELCH

48
What Will the Neighbors Say?

You cannot select a target in a vacuum. Those around you are going to react to what you do. Your rivals are also looking for their best opportunities to advance, ideally to your detriment.

As you apply the rules of aiming to evaluating your own opportunities, you simultaneously apply those same rules to predict what others around you should do. As you select the one best task for yourself, you must calculate what those around you are most likely going to do, either as you make your move or in response to it.

As you aim, you cannot see opportunities from your viewpoint; you must also imagine what it looks like to aim from others' viewpoints.

AIM

Strategy Is Like Chess

Aim requires thinking like a chess master. Before you move, you must consider your opponent's likely responses. You must:

- Examine all possible responses
- Avoid creating openings

Strategy insists that you consider the needs of others.

Only by foreseeing the possible moves of others can you create positions that others cannot easily attack.

You must not:

- Let others predict your plan
- Let others push you into moves

Or Is Strategy Like Poker?

Remember, you control other people by controlling their perceptions. People get information from what you do. What you say matters much less than the moves you make. When you choose a move, you are choosing to tell people something about yourself.

Strategy says movement **is** communication.

You must think like a poker player sitting at a table. It doesn't matter what you say at the poker table; the other players judge your position by how much you bet. They also judge by the way you act. What do your actions tell your opponents, and how will they respond?

- Know what it looks like you are doing.
- Know when others expect looks to be deceiving.

A man noticed a dog sitting with six gamblers at a poker table. Curious, he came closer and saw that there were cards and chips in front of the dog.

The next hand was dealt and cards were dealt to the dog. Then the dog took his turn with all the other players, calling, raising, discarding—everything the human players were doing. None of the other players seemed to pay any mind to the fact that they were playing with a dog.

Finally the man could no longer hold his tongue. He quietly commented to one of the players, "I can't believe that dog is playing poker. He must be the smartest dog in the world!"

The player smiled and said, "He isn't that smart. Every time he gets a good hand he wags his tail."

49 PROTECTING YOUR DOWNSIDE

Success over time comes from advancing to new positions. Defense, that is, maintaining the advantages of your existing position, only works over the short term, but for that period of time it is essential. Progress is like climbing a ladder. As you move from one rung to the next, you rely on your current position to secure the next. Aim enables you to make the best possible choices about when to defend and when to advance.

You start your defense as part of claiming your position, but you must continue to defend as long as you hold a position. As the situation changes, you must adjust your defense to make sure that you are secure.

Strategists know when to hold on and when to let go.

THE KEY TO DEFENSE: You must defend until you are certain you can advance.

Climbing the Ladder

Knowing when to move forward is no different than climbing a ladder.

If you need both hands and both feet to hold on to your existing position, you must stay where you are. You must have a free hand or foot to move up the ladder. You aim at advancing only if you have a surplus of resources. If you don't have more resources than you need to secure your existing position, you cannot even consider a move that takes you forward.

As you climb, others will try to go around you, take your rung away from you, or push you back down. If you cannot hold onto your existing position, you are usually forced back.

You cannot overreach yourself. Even an opening is dangerous if it tempts you into moving before you are secure.

Testing the Next Rung

If you have more resources than you need to hold your existing place, you can aim at advancing, but you don't move just because you have the resources to do so. You also need:

- ☑ Conditions favoring an advance
- ☑ An easy, safe place to move
- ☑ A new position with better future possibilities

Advances are seldom as simple as they seem at first. At the Pearly Gates, a bureaucrat was met by St. Peter. St. Peter gave him a piece of chalk and told the man that he must climb a ladder to reach heaven. On each rung, he had to write the name of someone he had held down in the organization rather than helped up. The bureaucrat started, writing, climbing, writing, climbing—hanging on with one hand while writing in chalk with the other. All of a sudden, something crushed the fingers on the hand he was holding on with. He looked up, and there, much to his surprise, was his boss coming down for more chalk.

"WE LIFT OURSELVES BY OUR THOUGHT, WE CLIMB UPON OUR VISION OF OURSELVES." ORISON SWETT MARDEN

50 Sometimes Things Are on the Level

Whether you choose to defend or advance depends heavily on the conditions in your environment. Strategy classifies decision-making conditions into four important categories.

Four Situations Affecting Aim

Four environmental situations determine your aim:

- **Level playing fields** are ideal conditions.
- **Change storms** are turbulent situations.
- **Indecision bogs** are murky situations.
- **Disparity mountains** are unbalanced situations.

Only when you are on a level playing field can you aim easily.

In change storms, where conditions are changing much more rapidly than normal, the rate of change destroys aim. In indecision bogs, positions are trapped in limbo. In disparity ranges, you are insecure about what you can control. What makes level playing fields different is that they are not turbulent, murky, or unbalanced.

Aim Under Ideal Conditions

You know you are on a level playing field when:

- ☑ Events are changing at their normal pace
- ☑ You are confident in the information you are getting
- ☑ The situation is not controlled by a few people

On a level playing field, you are free to choose. The situation does not force you to stay where you are or move. On a level playing field, you move forward when you have the resources. You may not choose to move if opportunities seem too risky or a better opportunity is certain to come along, but your general aim must be to move forward as quickly as possible.

THE KEY TO DECISION: **Choose the best imperfect alternative instead of waiting for perfection.**

Strategy is knowing both where to move and how to move.

A student asked his teacher, "What is love? How can I find it?"

The teacher answered, "Walk into that wheat field and pick only the most magnificent stalk, but you must know it when you see it. You cannot pick a stalk you passed if you don't find a better one."

The student walked into the field but returned empty-handed. He explained, "I found a magnificent stalk but I did not know if there were better ones ahead, so I didn't pick it. As I walked further, the stalks were not as good so I did not pick any in the end."

His teacher said, "And such is ideal love. Now, go into the forest and cut down the best tree without picking any you first passed by."

Before long, the student returned with a good but not perfect tree. His teacher asked, "Why that particular tree?"

The student answered, "Because last time I ended up with nothing. This was the first really good tree I saw. I chopped it because I did not want to miss the opportunity again."

His teacher then said, "And such is real love. At first, love is an ideal whose worth you don't appreciate until it's gone. Real love is learning to appreciate and live happily with your choices."

51 Blinded by Change Storms

Every situation changes, but some situations are so turbulent that you cannot take proper aim.

The pace of change is increasing everywhere, and there are many situations that *normally* change faster than others. For example, younger people go through more changes than older people.

It is another strategic paradox. Decision-making depends on good information. Good information is easier to get in stable situations. However, opportunity depends on change. Faster-changing situations create more opportunities than stable ones.

AIM

No matter what the normal pace of change in a given area, any situation can undergo a dramatic *temporary* increase in the pace of change. We call these conditions "change storms."

Strategists know when to wait.

Change storms can take many forms. Personal change storms can arise from death, divorce, a move to a new town, marriage, the birth of a child, and so on. In organizations, change storms arise with new management, mergers, and downsizing.

Aim to Stay out of Change Storms

After fourteen years of running a software company, I woke up to the fact that the climate in high tech was prone to continuous change storms. You have heard of dog years; high-tech companies age in rat years. In three years, most are dead.

When my wife and I sold our share in the software company, we moved away from change storms. We began giving seminars and publishing books on strategy based on the principles of Sun Tzu's *The Art of War.* We figured that anything that had been popular for 2,500 years was solid and dependable enough for anyone.

During Change Storms

During storms, change overwhelms information. You cannot pick a target.

Fortunately, these situations are easy to recognize. Storms of change are bright red flags. They stand out like thunder and lightning.

In the midst of a storm:

- You defend you current position if you possibly can
- If you cannot defend, move away from the storm
- You never advance into the storm
- Wait; the storm will pass

Change storms are dangerous. They create vulnerabilities that you cannot foresee. They spawn dangers that make defense the imperative. When your current position is caught in a change storm, you have to devote all your resources to defending yourself.

If the change storm destroys your existing position, you have to move, picking the best opening you can find. When you move, you always move away from the storm.

"THE ART OF PROGRESS IS TO PRESERVE ORDER AMID CHANGE." A. N. WHITEHEAD

52 Mired in Indecision Bogs

You can get trapped in a strategic limbo called an indecision bog. Some people are mired by their own indecision. Others get sucked in by the indecision of others.

Growing Worse With Time

Unlike change storms, which go away if you wait, indecisions bogs are created by too much waiting. Aim is the decision to improve your position. Some people are afraid of decisions because they do not come with guarantees. Indecision is a way of running away from problems. It is the choice of a slower but more painful and certain form of failure than making bad decisions.

AIM

Strategists know when they must move.

Unresolved Situations

Many critical decisions remain unresolved for long periods of time. Couples live together but do not marry. Young people attend college but never graduate. Companies are up for sale, but they are never sold. New employees are hired, but their responsibilities are never made clear.

Recognizing Indecision

Indecision bogs are more dangerous than change storms because they are more difficult to identify. Storms are noisy, disruptive, uncontrollable, and hard to miss. Bogs are quiet and serene on the surface, but they are all the more treacherous because they wait so patiently to suck you in and suck the life out of you.

People trapped in them are quiet—too quiet. When an important decision goes unmade, it also goes unmentioned. People avoid talking about their relationships when their relationships aren't going anywhere. If you hear anything coming out of an indecision bog, it is usually a lot of hemming and hawing.

The Challenge of Uncertainty

Indecision bogs represent the maximum of uncertainty. The lack of decision is bad enough, but the silence gives you very little information about what is really going on. Even when you are in them, you cannot tell immediately what is wrong.

The key is avoiding getting trapped by indecision:

- Never advance into situations that are too quiet.
- Move away or through indecisive situations quickly.
- Find islands of small, solid decisions when stuck.

Indecision is not a form of keeping your options open. You cannot get trapped in indecision bogs. You must make the key decisions that hold you. If you are trapped by the indecision of others, you must either force them into a decision or get away from them.

"THE GREATEST LOSS OF TIME IS DELAY AND EXPECTATION, WHICH DEPEND UPON THE FUTURE. WE LET GO THE PRESENT, WHICH WE HAVE IN OUR POWER, AND LOOK FORWARD TO THAT WHICH DEPENDS UPON CHANCE, AND SO RELINQUISH A CERTAINTY FOR AN UNCERTAINTY." SENECA

53 Climbing Mountains of Disparity

Can you take aim in situations where you do not completely control your fate? What happens when much more powerful people and organizations dominate your situation?

Mountains of disparity separate people in terms of power. You can work in a large organization, where decisions are made up in the hierarchy. Or you can get in conflict with the government. Or you can get in a one-sided relationship.

A Different Sort of Challenge

Like change storms, the mountains of disparity are easy to spot. You are in the mountains when you experience the following:

When you take a long time to finish, you are slow. When your boss takes a long time, he is thorough.

When you don't do it, you are lazy. When you boss does not do it, he is busy.

When you do something without being told, you are out of line. When your boss does the same, he takes the initiative.

When you make a mistake, you are an idiot. When your boss makes a mistake, he's only human.

When you are out of the office, you are wandering around. When your boss is out of the office, he's on business.

When you do well, your boss never remembers. When you do poorly, he never forgets.

It Is Up to You

Like indecision bogs, the mountains do not disappear if you wait. However, unlike bogs, these situations also do not get worse with time. These situations rely totally on your actions.

The main effect of disparity is psychological. You know:

- You have inferior information
- You cannot fight giants

This makes you feel inadequate.

Strategists know how to move when they are in another's shadow.

The truth is:

- ☑ Giants have their own concerns.
- ☑ Few of their decisions affect you.
- ☑ The power of others can work for you as readily as against you.

Disparity alone does not affect your ability to advance your position. You cannot control many aspects of your environment, but you can still make progress. What you cannot control, you work around or use.

Making Progress in Mountains

The secrets of working in disparate situations are:

- Keep out of the way of the powerful when possible.
- Never take a position against the powerful.
- Use opportunity to get the powerful on your side.

"IN CRITICAL MOMENTS EVEN THE VERY POWERFUL HAVE NEED OF THE WEAKEST." AESOP

AIM

54
In Praise of the Cheapskates

If you are in a situation that either forces or allows you to move forward, the next job of aim is to pick the best possible move forward. Picking the best possible move starts with a simple idea.

> THE KEY OF PARSIMONY: **You must control costs because you cannot predict rewards.**

Remember that strategy defines success as making advances that pay. A good advance always returns more value than it costs. The best advance returns the most value for the least expenditure of resources. However, there is a problem with this formula.

AIM

Strategists study costs carefully.

- Predictions of value are usually overestimated.
- Predictions of cost are always underestimated.

The truth is:

- ☑ You do not know the value of a move until long after.
- ☑ All moves will cost more than you expect.

To address these problems, strategy defines the best move as:

- The step that obviously has the least costs as long as that step takes you toward your goal
- The step that is the shortest and quickest

Get out of the Guessing Game

Strategy makes progress certain in the long run, but the long run is best served by managing costs in the short run. Most moves do little to improve your position. Minimizing the time, effort, and resources in making a move automatically minimizes your risks.

Strategic decisions are never just guesses.

Strategy emphasizes the measurable economic costs in making a move because you can easily fool yourself about the benefits. It is always a mistake to use unknown potential rewards to justify choosing one opening over another. You must base aim on tangible realities.

The Smallness of Small

Strategy defines "small" in a very simple, practical way.

- Small is measured in distance.
- Small is measured in the number of people affected.
- Small is measured in the time an advance takes.

For the sake of simplicity, we refer to these three categories of cost as distance, multitude, and duration. Each of these factors affects both the cost of making a given move and the potential problems encountered in making any particular move.

> "THE COST OF A THING IS THE AMOUNT OF WHAT I CALL LIFE WHICH IS REQUIRED TO BE EXCHANGED FOR IT, IMMEDIATELY OR IN THE LONG RUN." HENRY DAVID THOREAU

55
FAR IS FOUL

Distance is not just a measurement of space in strategy. More often in strategy, distance measures how much work you must do to get from one place to another. It is a measure of effort and difficulty.

Four Aspects of Distance

You can use the four external aspects of your position—the ground, climate, command, and systems—to think about various forms that distance can take.

Strategists count effort as a form of distance.

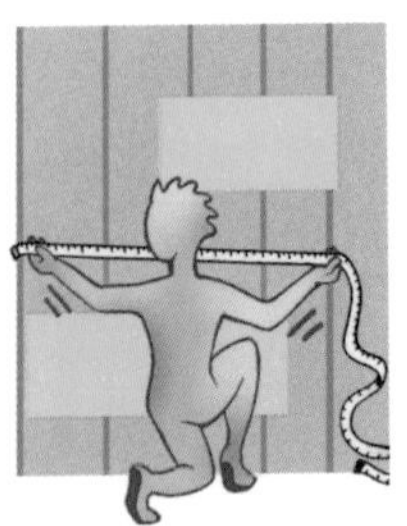

- Distance is space.
- Distance is change.
- Distance is new knowledge.
- Distance is new skills.

Transportation and Communication

Distance is an inescapable cost in making any advance. It affects two forms of costs:

- ☑ Transportation—the cost of moving between places
- ☑ Communication—the cost of passing messages

Don't Forget the Magical Twist!

Simplification tells you that moves over empty ground are always shorter than moves over full ground. Emptiness shortens distance. Fullness lengthens it.

AIM

The Shortest Distance

The ideal moves forward are always local ones, covering only a short distance. These positions are close both physically and mentally to where you are now.

Space Is Between the Ears

Physical distance is easy to compare. A move from New York to New Jersey is shorter than a move from New York to California. Comparing other forms of distance is a challenge. For example, any move from one job to another entails a change in climate, a change in character, and changes in systems. Moving from a sales job to a job as an assembly line worker is a bigger change than moving from selling to one group of customers to selling to different customers.

Emotion and perceptions are critical to strategy. The psychological differences between positions are more emotionally difficult to negotiate than most people suppose. Psychological distances are:

- Difficult to evaluate before you experience them
- Easy to overlook and underestimate in analysis

Psychological changes are especially difficult because other people don't understand what you are going through. As you move toward others, they see your position as more normal.

A man on a journey came to a broad river. He saw a woman standing on the opposite bank.

"Hello!" he called across. "How do I get to the other side?"

The woman just looked at him and started laughing.

"What's so funny?" the man asked.

"You are on the other side," the woman called back.

56
More Is Worse

When the first book on strategy was written 2,500 years ago, its primary focus was to dispel the misconception that size equals strength. According to the rules of emptiness and fullness, large crowds create weakness rather than strength.

Strategy considers the costs of alliances.

Problems With the Multitude

Crowds demonstrate strategic relativity at work. Size is fullness, and it creates weakness, especially in moving to new positions.

The larger the group:

- The more expensive the move
- The more complicated the move
- The more problems it causes

The smaller the group, the quicker it can move. Big is strong, but small is fast. This ability to move quickly explains why small organizations are on the forefront of new technologies while large organizations usually lag behind.

The Downside of Connections

Even moves that you make on your own affect many other people. The better connected you are in the world, the more people depend on you, and the more a change in your life affects other lives. Connections are another strategic strength, but, as with every other fullness, they create weakness. Connections increase your inertia, making any move more difficult.

When you move, you affect everyone you leave behind, and you affect everyone you move toward. If you change jobs, you affect the current people you work with and the people with whom you plan to work. These connections, uncontrolled, can inhibit progress.

The heaviest known element was recently discovered. The new element, named Bureaucracesium, has no protons or electrons. However, it does have one neutron, 125 assistant neutrons, 75 vice neutrons, and 111 assistant vice neutrons. These 312 particles are held together in a nucleus by a force that involves the continuous exchange of particles called morons.

Since it has no electrons, Bureaucracesium is totally inert. However, it can be detected chemically, since it impedes every reaction it comes into contact with. A tiny amount of Bureaucracesium caused one reaction to take over four days to complete; the normal reaction time is less than one second.

Bureaucracesium has a normal half-life of three years, at which time it does not decay, but undergoes a reorganization in which neutrons, vice neutrons, and assistant vice neutrons exchange places. Its mass increases after each reorganization.

Research indicates that Bureaucracesium occurs naturally. It tends to concentrate in certain areas, such as governmental agencies, large corporations, and universities. It is always found in the newest and most expensive buildings.

Bureaucracesium is known to be toxic at any level of concentration and can easily destroy any productive reactions where it is allowed to accumulate. Attempts are being made to determine how Bureaucracesium can be controlled to prevent irreversible damage, but the results to date are not promising.

57
Longer Is Wronger

Success requires using your time as effectively as possible. What happens when you pick a move that can drag on a long time?

- The costs mount; payback grows more distant.
- The world changes; the original goalposts move.
- You are tied up; you miss new opportunities.

Success means making advances pay. The more time an advance requires, the less likely it is to pay off. Those who do not calculate their time into their costs are always disappointed.

A man climbed to the top of Mt. Sinai to talk to God.

Standing on the mountaintop, he shouted to the sky, "Lord, what does a million years mean to you?"

To the man's surprise, God replied, "A minute."

The man thought for a moment and then asked, "And what does a million dollars mean to you?"

God replied, "A penny."

Smiling, the man asked, "Can I have a penny?"

God replied, "In a minute."

The chances of failure mount dramatically as time passes. Resistance and problems increase over time just like costs do.

Long, drawn-out moves eat new opportunities for lunch. Large, time-consuming advances that "succeed" technically reach their goal only in theory. They cannot pay back the time lost and especially the cost of the opportunities that are missed.

An Invitation to Quick Failure

Quick failures are much preferable to advances that are completed long after their value has expired. It is easier to recover from, learn from, and adjust to a failure.

Stategists test all their ideas to keep from wasting time.

Speed, Space, and Crowds

There is a close connection between distance, large groups, and speed.

- More distance takes longer to travel.
- Larger groups move more slowly.
- Speed requires local moves involving the fewest possible people.

Speed in the Progress Cycle

Listening takes time as you wait for opportunities, but speed is key in the next three steps of the Progress Cycle:

- When you aim, you must make quick decisions.
- You complete these moves as quickly as possible.
- You must quickly make your claim to get rewarded.

Delay in any of these three steps increases the chances of failure. The faster you finish one Progress Cycle, the faster you can start a new Progress Cycle. The faster your cycle time, the more powerful the tools of strategy become.

"THERE ARE NO SPEED LIMITS ON THE ROAD TO EXCELLENCE." DAVID W. JOHNSON

"THE SPEED OF THE BOSS IS THE SPEED OF THE TEAM." LEE IACOCCA

58
Oh, the Pain, the Pain

Each position is a stepping-stone to your next position. When you aim, you must foresee problems you might create for yourself in making a specific move. There are three general categories of problems:

Strategists foresee the problems in each course.

- Climate hazards
- Internal hazards
- Ground hazards

Pains of Time

Climate hazards arise from change. Changes in climate challenge both the ability to aim and the ability to move. Time affects aim and movement very differently. As time passes, targets move out of sight. As time passes, movements bog down.

Pains of Organization

Internal hazards pit organization against mission. Systems and command grow to obstruct a mission rather than support it. Command leads to ego. Systems lead to rigid rules. Both can overpower mission instead of supporting it.

Most Importantly: Pains of Space

Ground hazards are more complicated. Space is three-dimensional and creates three kinds of problems, called dangers, distances, and obstacles.

- **Dangers** are sticking points.
- **Distances** are space problems.
- **Obstacles** are passing problems.

Dangers create problems moving out of positions. Distances make it difficult to move into a position and defend it. Obstacles make it difficult to get into a new position but simplify defending a position. One position's obstacle is another position's defense. People are helped and hurt by obstacles.

Dangers, distances, and obstacles also increase the costs of getting anywhere.

Stategy sees the ground's three dimensions in danger, distance, and obstacles.

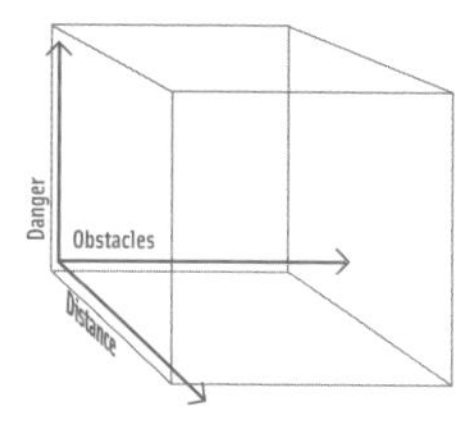

Consider the car that got stuck in a muddy country road. The driver paid a nearby farmer fifty dollars to pull him out.

"At those prices, I should think you would be pulling people out of the mud night and day," said the motorist.

"Can't," bragged the farmer. "At night I have to haul water for the hole in the road."

"I DON'T BELIEVE IN INTUITION. WHEN YOU GET SUDDEN FLASHES OF PERCEPTION...YOU'VE BEEN GETTING READY TO KNOW IT FOR A LONG TIME, AND WHEN IT COMES, YOU FEEL YOU'VE KNOWN IT ALWAYS." KATHERINE ANNE PORTER

Strategy teaches that avoiding hazards is easier than dealing with them.

AIM

59 STICKING AND GETTING STUCK

Since strategy depends on continual progress, danger is defined as getting stuck so you cannot advance. The biggest danger in moving to a new position is that the position will make it harder, not easier, for you to make your next step forward. Any forethought keeps you out of situations that are a dead end, but there are two other types of dangers that are harder to foresee:

- ☑ **Peak positions** that lead to no further progress
- ☑ **One-way positions** to which you cannot return

AIM

Peaks: It's All Downhill From Here

You cannot move away from a peak position without losing ground. You don't just take a painless step back so you can make two steps forward from a peak position. You take ten steps backward and maybe never get back where you were.

Strategy keeps you on top of your position.

In 1985, Coca-Cola replaced its hundred-year-old drink formula that was regularly beaten in taste tests against its competitor, Pepsi. The new formula beat Pepsi consistently in tests, but it was a market disaster. The original formula was on a peak and the people at Coke didn't realize they were advancing over a cliff.

When you are in a peak position, you are on top of your area with no way of getting to a higher mountain next door without leaving your particular perch and risking everything. You can perhaps expand a peak position, but you cannot ever give it up.

You can aim at a peak position. Many people do. But be careful what you wish for. You are going to be there for a long, long time.

- You don't advance peak positions; you defend them.

One-Way and You Get One Chance

One-way positions are dangerous because when you leave these positions, you cannot return to them. This is dangerous because:

- You destroy these positions when you leave them
- Your advances out of these positions can fail
- If your advance fails, you lose everything

Like climbing a ladder, when you reach for the next rung, you hold on to the existing rung. If the new rung breaks, you don't want to fall.

Strategy is an exclusive club: everyone wants back in after they leave.

One-way positions are common. When you quit a job, you usually cannot go back if your new job doesn't work out. When you get a divorce, it destroys the relationship, usually making remarriage impossible.

- You get one chance to move out of a one-way position.
- You advance from it only when you are certain the advance will work.

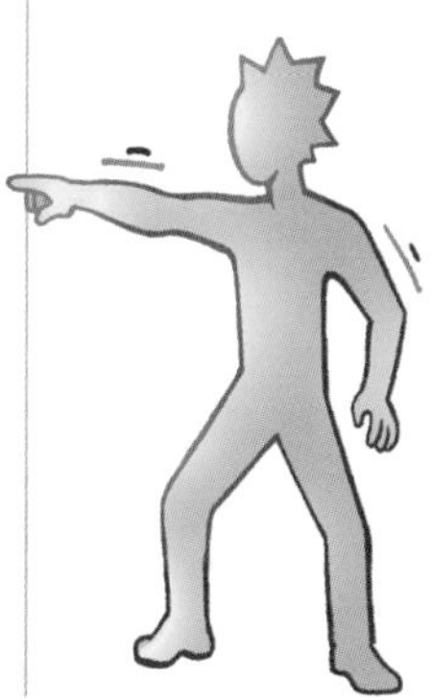

You can move into one-way streets. You often must. When you aim for them, you have to know exactly what you are doing.

AIM

60
Getting Too Loose and Get Tight Right

When you make an advance, you also have to ask yourself if the move is making your position more focused or less focused. Focus in aim and unity in movement are the primary sources of strategic force. When you look toward your desired position, you must question the amount of space available to you at the end of the move. Again, there are two extremes:

☑ **Spread-out positions** that stretch your resources
☑ **Constricted positions** of a limited size

AIM

Spreading the Love Too Thin

Growth in many different areas is not an inherently bad thing if those areas can be tied closely together. Problems arise when the areas in which you get involved are distant from one another, geographically or psychologically. If your position pulls you in different directions at once, you cannot defend it.

Strategists avoid spreading themselves out.

Spread-out positions are:

- A strain on limited resources
- The source of many openings
- An invitation to opponents

You have only a certain amount of resources. More territory can theoretically generate more resources, but your time is always limited. You can juggle only so many balls at a time. Add one ball too many and they all come crashing down. Spread-out positions are weak because they invite attack. Big territories are hard to defend. They leave too many openings for your opponents to attack you.

The secret in growing or expanding your territory:

- Keep it all closely tied together.

Filling It Up

The opposite of a spread-out position is a constricted position. A constricted position is of a limited size. The proverbial big fish in a small pond is in a constricted position. So are key employees in small companies.

Strategists continually narrow their focus over time.

With constricted positions, you must:

- Be the first to find them
- Fill them completely
- Never attack others in them

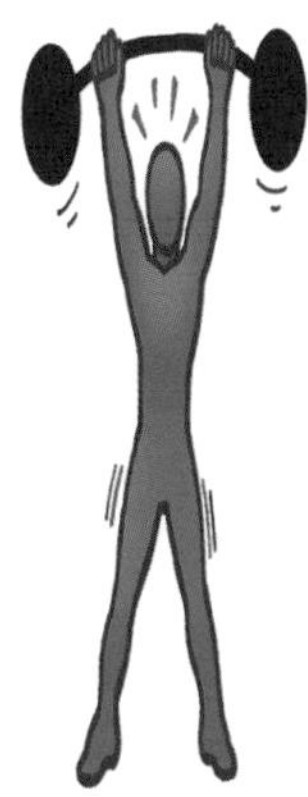

These positions allow whoever holds them to dominate naturally and easily. A spouse in a marriage is in a constricted position. A company with a unique product targeted at a small market is also in a constricted position. Niches are easy to defend if you fill them. You are only vulnerable if you do not commit yourself. For example, a spouse who takes marriage for granted is not filling his or her position.

"PERCEPTION IS STRONG AND SIGHT WEAK. IN STRATEGY IT IS IMPORTANT TO SEE DISTANT THINGS AS IF THEY WERE CLOSE AND TO TAKE A DISTANCED VIEW OF CLOSE THINGS." MIYAMOTO MUSASHI

61
It Has to Be Hard to Be Good

Future positions are also defined by the number of obstacles that surround them. Obstacles are natural barriers that make moving into these positions difficult. Barriers to entry can be physical, but more often they are psychological and mental. The most common barrier to entry is a lack of knowledge.

Again, there are two extremes to obstacles.

- ☑ **Unobstructed positions** have very few obstacles.
- ☑ **Barricaded positions** have a great many obstacles.

It's Hard When It's Good

You take the bad with the good. Unobstructed positions are:

- Easy to get into
- Hard to defend

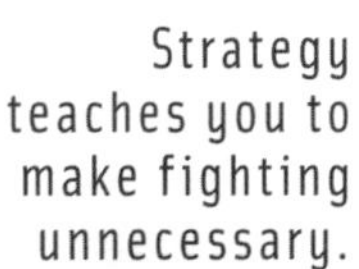

There are always openings into unobstructed positions. That *is* what makes them unobstructed. These common openings are tempting, but they are tricky to use.

Their lack of any barriers is an invitation to trouble. If you can move into a new territory easily, others can move into that territory easily as well. These positions are easy to acquire, but they are impossible to defend. This dramatically decreases the value of these positions.

Unobstructed positions allow you to move forward easily, and you usually are forced out of them because others move so easily. It's like a relationship with someone who is "playing the field." Yes, you can get into the relationship very easily. However, the position is limited. You are soon going to be replaced by someone new.

It's Good When It's Hard

Barricaded positions are the opposite extreme.

- Hard to get into
- Easy to defend

Getting into a barricaded position usually requires a whole campaign. The whole principle of campaigns is that they are required to get around barriers. This makes these positions costly and time-consuming to acquire.

Once you are in these positions, those barriers to entry protect you. You are secure. The benefit of the ground is yours alone without having to fight off competitors.

Good strategy is the key that lets you in and keeps others out.

THE KEY OF OPPORTUNISM: **You always use unique openings to circumvent barriers to entry.**

Strategy is opportunistic. The best opportunity of all is when you find a rare key that gives you easy entry into a barricaded position. If a position is difficult to achieve when it is empty, it is invulnerable once you have filled it.

"IF YOU CAN FIND A PATH WITH NO OBSTACLES, IT PROBABLY DOESN'T LEAD ANYWHERE." FRANK A. CLARK

62
THE "PREPARING EXPECTATIONS" GAME

This final step of aim is a little like judging which way the wind is blowing before you pull the trigger. It is critical in hitting your target but takes a great deal of good judgment. After you decide the best opportunity to pursue, you have a difficult decision to make:

> THE KEY TO PREPARATION: **You must tell people your aims only if it is required to get rewarded.**

There are two conflicting issues:

- You need the support of others to make a change.
- Some will create problems if they know your aims.

What Game Are You Playing?

You must aim at making a claim. In the end, you need people to recognize what you have done. Different moves have different requirements in terms of getting recognized and rewarded.

- ☑ Some opportunities are like playing pool.
- ☑ Other opportunities are like poker.
- ☑ Some opportunities are like hide-and-seek.

When an opportunity is like pool, you have to call your shot for it to count. If you do not call the shot, everyone assumes that what happened was an accident and you will not get credit for it.

When an opportunity is like poker, you signal what you hold, but even after the hand is over, people don't know what you were holding unless they pay to see your hand. People judge only by what they see, knowing that the complete story is hidden.

When the game is like hide-and-seek, the only way you succeed is by keeping everything a secret until you make your claim at the end. If people see what you are doing, you automatically lose the game. You can only win if the result is a complete surprise.

Strategists control expectations to control the show.

The "Preparing Expectations" Game

When you aim at a specific move, you need to play a little game with yourself. It's like setting the table for a meal, but this game prepares everyone for what is about to come. The steps are easy:

First, ask yourself if anyone absolutely needs to know what you intend in order for your move to get rewarded at the end.

If the answer is yes, determine the minimum information that you must share to gain the needed cooperation and recognition.

Now, ask yourself how others might make your move difficult if they know what you intend and why they might work against you.

Next, think about ways that you might prepare the information to satisfy the first group and mislead the second.

You win the "Preparing Expectations" game when supporters are excited while opponents are confused.

"LUCK IS WHAT HAPPENS WHEN PREPARATION MEETS OPPORTUNITY." SENECA

AIM

63
The Keys to Aiming

- When you aim, you must choose only moves that clearly advance your mission.
- Aim at advances that focus your efforts on the single best activity and lock out distractions.
- Aim at ordinary advances, but think how they might be rearranged to create extraordinary break-throughs.
- Foresee how others might counter your moves.
- Advance when your position is secure and you have more resources than you need to defend it.
- Defend during change storms, move from indecision bogs, and don't fear the mountains of disparity.
- Aim at making short, small, quick advances rather than long, big, slow advances.
- Before aiming at a new position, consider how it will position you for future advances.
- Fill tight spaces instead of getting spread out.
- Move quickly in and out of unobstructed spaces and get into barricaded spaces however you can.
- Prepare people's expectations to create a maximum of reward and a minimum of resistance.

Part V
Move to Pursue the Opportunity

MOVE

64
Drifting Is Not Moving

A "move" is any action—anything you say or do—to change your position. Sometimes, you can change people's perceptions with a single word. More often, it takes a series of actions—a real change in behavior—to change your position.

Strategy teaches how to get the most from every effort.

Many people think that they create good impressions with other people by being agreeable and doing what those other people want. This is the opposite of what happens in real life. People respect and support those who are leaders and take control of their lives.

MOVE

Adrift in a Sea of Trouble

Many people sit in their current positions like life preservers. As they drift down the river of life, they curse their luck as they bump into problem after problem. These people hear about a good job but don't go to the interview. They see someone they are attracted to, but they never make a date. They pick the winners at the racetrack, but they never buy a ticket. These people never lose, but they also never win.

- Drifting is not the path of least resistance.
- Drifting is the path of least control.
- People choose not to pursue opportunities.

The Costs and Benefits of Fear

"Moving to a new position" translates in everyday terms to changing some aspect of our lives. Every advance either creates a new relationship or changes an old one. Changing how we act is frightening because it moves us into unexplored territory.

Fear is natural and can even be beneficial. Command requires courage, but one of the defects of command is fearlessness. Change is not a choice. The changing climate alone dictates that your situation is going to change. The only way it is going to change for the better is if you control your own destiny.

Action is a choice, but success requires movement with a purpose. You cannot reach your goals if you don't stretch yourself.

- Be eager and restless for change.
- Be ready to move at any time.

Many of your moves will not be successful, but when you use strategy, you quickly put your mistakes behind you.

A woman lost her job and prayed, "God, please help me win the lotto. I've lost my job, and if I don't win, I will lose my house."

The woman didn't win, but she tried again. "God, I've lost my job, my house, and if I don't win the lotto now, I'll lose my car."

Again someone else won and again she prayed, "My God, I've lost my business, my house, and my car. Now my children are going hungry. I don't often ask you for help. PLEASE just let me win the lotto this one time so I can get my life back in order."

Suddenly there was a blinding flash of light as the heavens opened and the woman heard the voice of God: "You just have to meet Me halfway on this. Buy a lottery ticket."

65
The Quick and the Dead

Aim determines the best opening to pursue, but your skill at moving determines whether or not you can catch it. People make three mistakes in moving to a new position.

- They take too long.
- They concentrate too few resources.
- They come into conflict with others.

Not getting started is the first problem. A woman moved to a new state with a different climate and asked the local nurseryman how long it took for tomatoes to grow and get ripe in that area.

"Are you planting today?" asked the nurseryman.

"I don't know exactly when I'll plant," admitted the woman.

"Then I can't tell you," said the nurseryman.

"Why not?" asked the woman.

"Well, if you plant today," explained the nurseryman, "it takes sixty days for tomatoes to ripen, but if you plant tomorrow, it's sixty-one. Two weeks from now, more than seventy-four 'cause days are shorter. Wait a month, and they'll never get ripe."

When you take too long to move, the opportunity passes you by. Every minute you delay in taking action makes success less and less likely. When you move without putting all your resources into it, you also increase your chances of failure and opposition. If you are the leader, you unite your team to move.

You must avoid conflict with other people. Move into emptiness, away from the crowd. The more opposition you face, the less likely success becomes.

Strategists seek new areas away from the crowd.

A Moving Experience

- Move to new positions quickly and out of old areas slowly.
- Focus all available resources to make the move a success.
- Use detours as your highway.

Never give up your old position until the new one is secured. Halfhearted moves are much more likely to fail. Concentrate all available resources on the current move to make sure it succeeds.

Everyone expects you to take direct routes. If you go after what you want directly, people will know where you are going and will be tempted to oppose you. Indirect routes disguise your intentions and discourage opposition.

Strategy takes you where no one else thinks to go.

"THERE WAS AN IMMEASURABLE DISTANCE BETWEEN THE QUICK AND THE DEAD: THEY DID NOT SEEM TO BELONG TO THE SAME SPECIES; AND IT WAS STRANGE TO THINK THAT BUT A LITTLE WHILE BEFORE THEY HAD SPOKEN AND MOVED AND EATEN AND LAUGHED." W. SOMERSET MAUGHAM

66
Great Spirits and Small Minds

Who can explain why people are so contrary?

The Key to Resistance: **If others know you are making a move, some will try to stop you.**

The people who try to stop you may be your opponents, but they can also be your friends or even complete strangers. This is the "turn signal" rule. If you signal before you change lanes, some people just have to speed up and cut you off. This doesn't get them where they are going any faster. Humans just can't resist the temptation to block each other when they have the opportunity.

Razzle-Dazzle Them

You can prevent people from stopping you if you:

- Create a puzzle
- Use misdirection
- Keep your move a secret

You create a puzzle by breaking a move to a new position into pieces. If others cannot see how the pieces fit together, they cannot block you. This is the technique used in chess.

If you can make one type of move look like another, people will still try to stop you, but they will oppose the wrong things. Betting in poker is based on misdirection.

Of course, secrecy is best. If others do not notice that you are making a move, they do not even think to stop you.

It Is Easier to Ask Forgiveness

You want to get into your new position before anyone knows how to oppose your move. This allows you to defend your position rather than fight your way into it.

Strategy teaches fight avoidance.

It is always easier to defend than attack. Once you are in your new position, most people will lose their strange, inexplicable desire to oppose you.

Advancing and developing positions that are impossible to attack—and that make others want to join you—is the basis of all strategy.

Defense can use misdirection as well. For example, a lawyer defending a man accused of burglary tried this creative defense: "My client merely inserted his arm into the window and removed a few trifling articles. His arm is not himself, and I fail to see how you can punish the whole individual for an offense committed by his limb."

"Well put," the judge replied. "Using your logic, I sentence the defendant's arm to one year's imprisonment. He can accompany it or not, as he chooses."

The defendant smiled. And, with his lawyer's assistance, he detached his artificial limb, laid it on the bench, and walked out.

MOVE

"GREAT SPIRITS HAVE ALWAYS ENCOUNTERED VIOLENT OPPOSITION FROM MEDIOCRE MINDS." ALBERT EINSTEIN

67
Flow Like Water and Change Like Wind

You can know exactly where the position you desire is located, but you cannot plan exactly how to get there. The sea of human activity is more like a restless ocean than a fixed grid of city streets.

THE KEY OF ADAPTABILITY: **All moves depend totally on your ability to adapt.**

No Crystal Ball

You cannot know the conditions you will face getting to your destination until you are on your way. Like a ship sailing across the ocean, you must continually adapt to the changing winds and currents using all the techniques of sailing. In strategy, you must continually adapt to the changing winds and currents of situations using all the techniques of moving.

Strategy makes you acutely aware of changes around you.

MOVE

As you advance in life, you are going to meet many different conditions on the way to many different destinations. Some moves will be pleasant excursions. Other moves will turn into crazy games of chicken. Some moves will become races. In other moves, you will discover that the way you planned to go has been closed for construction.

"ADAPT OR PERISH, NOW AS EVER, IS NATURE'S INEXORABLE IMPERATIVE." H. G. WELLS

The Nine Specific Conditions

There are nine special situations that you must instantly recognize and adapt to:

- **Scattering conditions** arise when attacked by a foe.
- **Easy conditions** arise early in a new advance.
- **Disputed conditions** arise on valuable ground.
- **Open conditions** arise when the ground is clear.
- **Shared conditions** arise where paths converge.
- **Bad conditions** arise when your path is difficult.
- **Dangerous conditions** arise deep in hostile areas.
- **Tight conditions** arise when you have few options.
- **Desperate conditions** arise when you face failure.

The Nine Maneuvers

Seeing your situation, you must make exactly the right maneuver to address it. You don't sail the same in a storm as you do when the weather is clear. Strategy teaches nine basic maneuvers in response to different specific conditions that you encounter:

- **Diversion** is defense by invasion.
- **Taking** is getting as much as you can.
- **Blocking** obstructs a rival's progress.
- **Shadowing** is copying or following others.
- **Alliance** is joining with others.
- **Perseverance** is not stopping when facing difficulty.
- **Scrounging** is securing needed resources.
- **Surprise** is doing the unexpected.
- **Battle** is meeting opponents or challenges directly.

68
A Finishing School for Campaigns

As a series of advances that lead toward a longer-term goal, a campaign is a major strategic commitment. Finishing college, starting a business, winning a love, and writing a book—*hey, I'm doing that now*—are all various forms of campaigns.

A Beginning, Middle, and End

Campaigns have a beginning, a middle, and an end. Planning a wedding is a campaign because it has an end. Being married is not a campaign because ideally it has no end, well, other than death.

A good way to understand the nine specific conditions that you face in moving is seeing how they arise as stages within a larger campaign. All these conditions occur outside of campaigns, and they can also arise "out of order" within campaigns, but their normal sequence does help explain what these specific conditions are and why they recur so commonly.

MOVE

Beginnings Are Delicate Times

These first three conditions come early in a campaign:

☑ **Scattering conditions** come before you move, when threatened by a powerful opponent in your own territory.

☑ **Easy conditions** arise when you first move into a new area and the new project is exciting and full of promise.

☑ **Disputed conditions** occur on rich ground where people immediately come into conflict with each other.

The Gooey Middle

Strategy requires a beginning, middle, and end game.

Open, shared, and bad conditions occur in the middle of a campaign, after the campaign has become more developed.

☑ **Open conditions** are when everyone can advance at the same time.

☑ **Shared conditions** arise when you and noncompetitors can cooperate on working toward the same goals.

☑ You meet **bad conditions** when the route you have chosen proves to be much more difficult than you expected.

To the End of the Line

All campaigns become more difficult and dangerous as you approach your goal.

☑ **Dangerous conditions** arise when a move goes on for a long time and opposition tries to choke off your resources.

☑ You get into **tight conditions** when you go through a transition that leaves you vulnerable to attack.

☑ Finally, you get into **desperate situations** where you have to risk everything in order to win your new position.

MOVE

> "ANY NEW VENTURE GOES THROUGH THE FOLLOWING STAGES: ENTHUSIASM, COMPLICATION, DISILLUSIONMENT, SEARCH FOR THE GUILTY, PUNISHMENT OF THE INNOCENT, AND DECORATION OF THOSE WHO DID NOTHING."
> ANONYMOUS

69 When Offense Is the Best Defense

Defending your existing position sometimes requires an advance into new areas. Defense is usually less expensive than an advance, but when you are targeted by an opponent who is powerful enough to overcome your defense, it creates a scattering condition.

When a powerful foe attacks, it "scatters" for two reasons.

☑ Your supporters abandon you.

☑ You must move to avoid the attack.

The Diversion Maneuver

Under these scattering conditions, you don't want to meet your opponent to fight over your position. If battle is about your position—your record, your history, your past actions, etc.—it is going to do damage.

The strategy is to divert enemies when you cannot face them.

Instead of defending yourself, you must identify an opening your opponent has left unguarded and move on it. Divert your enemy from his original purpose. Your goal is not to advance your position but to discourage the attack on your position.

Smaller Is Quicker

Diversion leverages size against speed. Powerful enemies have a lot of responsibilities that you can attack, moving from one to the next. Diversion isn't used against smaller, quicker opponents. You do not move when they attack you. You simply defend.

Avoid a Showdown

You never want to engage powerful people in battles. You just want to get their attention and respect. You use the diversion in such a way that it is clear that your goal is not to hurt or embarrass others. You are simply protecting your own position.

The success of diversion is based on it being unexpected. You don't threaten diversions. You quickly execute them, moving into the opponent's territory and then moving quickly from one place to another until a standoff is reached.

Diversion is often the simplest thing. A local busybody was the self-appointed monitor of a small town's morals. This woman made a habit of attacking others publicly for their failings. Many people in the community did not approve of her methods but feared becoming the target of her gossip so they maintained their silence.

She made a mistake, however, when she accused a new member of her church of being an alcoholic. She told the whole congregation that she had seen his old pickup parked in front of the town's only bar one afternoon. She said that everyone seeing it there would know exactly what he was up to.

The new member, a man of few words, didn't argue. He just turned and walked away.

Later that evening, the man who had been attacked quietly parked his pickup in front of the busybody's house.

70 Like Taking Candy From a Baby

When you pick the right opportunity, you can discover that success is easier than you expected. These easy conditions:

- ☑ Are more common when projects are new
- ☑ Are the result of good aim
- ☑ Result from openings with little or no opposition

The Taking Maneuver

When you meet easy conditions, you use the taking maneuver to go:

- As far as you can go
- As fast as you can go
- As long as you can go

MOVE

Just Don't Stop

You aim at short, quick, small advances, but you cannot take easy conditions for granted and stop too soon. Easy is usually a very temporary condition that ends too soon on its own.

While taking, you simply keep going until you run into barriers or opposition or start running low on resources. You advance your position as far as you can, using the easy conditions to expand your territory. As long as conditions remain easy, the situation is telling you that you haven't gone far enough.

Upon hearing my presentations on strategy, several large companies started asking me, "Couldn't you adapt these ideas for our marketing department?" "Couldn't you do a book for our managers?" Because I knew the principles so well, it was easy for me to create these adaptations on demand. The books were easy to sell and easy to write, so before I knew it, I had published a complete line of strategy books for career and business. It wasn't what I had planned, but it was too easy to stop.

When It Isn't Easy Anymore

Strategy teaches you to take the gifts you are given.

When you reach this condition's end, you must stop your advance. You stop when you encounter resistance. You stop when you run out of resources you can afford to invest. You stop when you run out of time. At that point, you go to the claim stage to evaluate the quality of your move and see what you have accomplished.

Communicate or Get in Trouble

There is only one important rule when you go into the taking mode. You need to let other people know what you are doing. Communication is important because you are going further and doing more than you expected. Your rapid advance is going to affect other people. If you don't keep people informed, these advances get you into trouble in the claim stage.

"PROGRESS ISN'T MADE BY EARLY RISERS. IT'S MADE BY LAZY MEN TRYING TO FIND EASIER WAYS TO DO SOMETHING." ROBERT HEINLEIN

71
Knocking and Blocking

When you find a desirable opening, others often discover the same opening at the same time. Disputed conditions arise:

- ☑ When there is an obviously desirable prize
- ☑ When access to that reward is limited

Desirable prizes are rare. Well-paying fun jobs get more applicants than poor-paying hard jobs. People naturally go after them. They bunch together like people getting tangled in a doorway.

Avoiding Conflict

In disputed conditions:

- You cannot attack your rivals
- You must discourage them from attacking you

Avoiding conflict is difficult when you face rivals for a desirable prize. You avoid attacks because while you are fighting with rivals, someone else who avoided the fight will sweep in and take the prize. If you are busy fighting, you make it impossible to block, which is the right maneuver for this situation.

Good strategy requires making friends with rivals.

The Blocking Maneuver

Under disputed conditions, you must block your rivals from winning the position that you desire. To block them, you must:

MOVE

- Get close to opponents' positions
- Learn their weaknesses
- Use their weaknesses to stop their progress

Blocking maneuvers use your closeness to your rivals against them. They work only if you first get close.

A successful businessman was the defendant in a lawsuit. Before the trial, he discussed the situation with his lawyer.

"In business, I always try to get people on my side," said the defendant. "Would it help if I sent the judge a box of cigars?"

"Oh no!" his lawyer cried. "It's the worst thing you could do. He is a stickler about ethics. You shouldn't even smile at him."

After thinking a moment, the businessman asked, "Would it hurt if I made friends with the plaintiff?"

"It won't help," his lawyer responded. "You can't dissuade him with a handshake and a smile, but I don't see how it could hurt."

So before the trial, the defendant went over to the plaintiff, shook his hand, patted his back, and exchanged business cards.

The businessman won the judgment, but his lawyer admitted, "That was a close thing. I don't really know how we won."

"I think it was the tip you gave me about the cigars," suggested the businessman. "I didn't dare smile at the judge."

"A good thing too," said his lawyer. "I'm sure we would have lost the case if you'd sent him those stupid cigars of yours."

"But I did send them," admitted the defendant.

"What? You did?" said the lawyer. "I don't understand."

"I sent the cigars," the businessman confessed. "But I enclosed the business card that the plaintiff gave me."

72
The Sincerest Form of Flattery

Open conditions are the opposite of disputed conditions. Disputed conditions bring people into conflict because they are going after the same, limited reward. In open conditions, many different people can make good progress without conflict.

Disputed conditions are defined by the narrowness of the opening, but open conditions are defined by the broadness of the opening. If disputed conditions are like a narrow doorway where people get tangled, open conditions are like a broad racetrack where any number of people can advance at the same time.

Open conditions arise when a move uncovers:

☑ A broad new territory

☑ More resources than competitors

It is like the opening of a new continent to exploration. Imagine the Asians coming across the ice to find North America empty, or, more recently, the creation of the Internet. All that territory means a lot of opportunities, but the goal is to get in position to stake out the best possible claims.

The Dark Lining in the Silver Cloud

The goal under open conditions is to make as much progress as possible, but the standards are different from those under easy conditions. Under easy conditions, you are alone. Under open conditions, your progress is measured against that of the people around you. Their progress becomes the measure of your own.

If you come out of open conditions with a position inferior to that of your competitors, you are in trouble. When conditions change—and the rules of climate tell us that they must change—your position is going to be very difficult to defend. Under open conditions, your position degrades quickly because everyone is advancing. If you don't move forward as quickly as everyone else, you are really falling behind. These situations not only encourage you to keep up with others; they demand it.

The Shadowing Maneuver

Under open conditions, the contest is like a race. The shadowing maneuver is simple:

- You identify the leaders.
- You keep with them.
- You copy everything they do.

Strategy teaches you when you can copy others most effectively.

Like race car drivers who conserve fuel by drafting behind their opponents, you shadow your opponents, using them to guide you and blaze the trail for you.

When shadowing, you copy all the best ideas of the leaders. You emulate them, copy them, and imitate them. By shadowing, you are sure to keep up. This puts you in a position to surpass the leaders when conditions become more limiting.

When shadowing, you stay in position to pull out a surprise.

"TO DO JUST THE OPPOSITE IS ALSO A FORM OF IMITATION." GEORG CHRISTOPH LICHTENBERG

73 The Kindness of Strangers

Under shared conditions, people can make better progress toward their different immediate goals by working with each other. In these situations, those who find the best allies the most quickly are going to be the most successful. Shared conditions arise when:

- ☑ People can work together for a shared reward
- ☑ They need each other's help to get that reward

There are many shared conditions in life. You want to play a game of golf, but the course doesn't allow lone players. The freeway is backed up, but the high-occupancy lane is empty and a hitchhiker is standing by the road. You can win a business contract, but you cannot provide all the types of services the contract requires.

The Alliance Maneuver

Making an alliance solves your problem. You join up with someone at the golf course with whom you can play a round. You pick up the hitchhiker to use the HOV lane. You find a temporary business partner who can provide the needed services so you can partner on the contract.

The Fastest Friends

Under shared conditions, you must:

- Instantly see the possibilities of partnership
- Act quickly to win a partner

Unless you are in the habit of looking at situations from the viewpoint of others, it often isn't obvious when you and a stranger share a common bond of self-interest. Most people don't see the possibilities of shared conditions because they are focused only on their own problems. They don't see the problems of others, especially when those problems—like the problems of the driver and the hitchhiker—are very different.

Under shared conditions, the first person to create an alliance usually wins. You must instantly act on the recognition. Someone else gets the only open tee time if he or she finds a golfing partner before you do. If someone picks up the hitchhiker before you do, they get to use the HOV lane and you don't. In a shared situation, time is of the essence.

The Danger of Shared Conditions

- You cannot trust temporary allies.
- You cannot lead temporary alliances.

You do not know these people. You have no longer-term commitment to each other. A pick-up golf partner might be a critic. The hitchhiker could be a serial killer.

If decisions have to be made, alliances generate a battle over authority. The good news is that you get the business contract. The bad news is that you and your temporary partner cannot agree on what satisfying the contract means.

Strategy sets guidelines for how far you can trust strangers.

74
When Winners Know Not to Quit

If all conditions were sunshine and light, strategy wouldn't be important. You wouldn't have to spend your good money on invaluable books such as the one you are reading and feel the strong subliminal need to recommend it to all your friends and relatives. Fortunately—for my book sales—the world is not all sunshine. The roadways ice up, the fog rolls in, rockfalls block the road, and your tires go flat. Bad conditions are common in every aspect of life.

- ☑ New barriers can arise at any time.
- ☑ Every substantial move encounters them.

If you expect trouble, you aren't going to be disappointed too often. The truth is that even short, small, quick moves can run into unexpected obstacles. The longer, larger, and slower the move, the more certain these difficulties become.

Obstacles are nature's little way of testing your character and your commitment to a goal.

MOVE

The Persistence Maneuver

The move isn't too complicated. Simply:

Don't stop.

"It does not matter how slowly you go so long as you do not stop." Confucius

When I first began seeing the wonderful woman who is now my wife, she wasn't interested in a relationship. She had been married, had her heart broken, and didn't see much benefit in it.

However, I found ways to spend time with her. As time went on, she would periodically decide that we were getting too close and break it off. However, I didn't give up. After a few weeks of separation I would call her. We would see each other again. We would get close again. After a few cycles of this, she had had enough.

"Enough. Either we break up forever or get married," she said.

We were married over twenty years ago and she still gives me a bad time about the fact that I wasn't the one who proposed.

You Control What Happens

Bad conditions can slow you down. They can force you to change your route. They can frustrate and anger you. What bad conditions cannot do is stop you. Only you can stop yourself.

Expect and prepare to meet obstacles. You may not see them when you start, but obstacles are always there. Your goal from the beginning must be to surmount them.

"NOTHING IN THE WORLD CAN TAKE THE PLACE OF PERSISTENCE. TALENT WILL NOT; NOTHING IS MORE COMMON THAN UNSUCCESSFUL MEN WITH TALENT. GENIUS WILL NOT; UNREWARDED GENIUS IS ALMOST A PROVERB. EDUCATION WILL NOT; THE WORLD IS FULL OF EDUCATED DERELICTS. PERSISTENCE AND DETERMINATION ALONE ARE OMNIPOTENT. THE SLOGAN 'PRESS ON' HAS SOLVED AND ALWAYS WILL SOLVE THE PROBLEMS OF THE HUMAN RACE."
CALVIN COOLIDGE

75 When You've Been a Long Time Gone

Any move that continues for a long time without getting you to a new, defensible position gets into dangerous conditions. Two things happen as a move goes on for a long time:

- You start to run out of resources.
- You create more and more opposition.

These two conditions often reinforce each other, especially within large organizations.

- Supporters become opponents as resources run out.
- Opponents work to cut off your resources.

Jumping off the Bandwagon

When a move takes too long, you must be concerned about running out of resources. Your move may have been a popular idea at first, but as time passes without it producing rewards, support from others evaporates. Popular ideas become pariahs if they don't pay off soon enough. People are quick to become critics.

Resources have a nasty habit of running out on you.

As economic pressures increase, your opponents start sniping at you. As time goes on, more and more people reflexively want to criticize and oppose you. This situation goes from bad to worse as your opponents try to cut off your resources.

People always feel justified in cutting you off. A pre-med student was told that his student loan would be cut unless he passed a physics course that he had already failed twice. His physics professor was lecturing on a particularly abstruse concept and the student rudely asked, "Why do we have to learn this stuff?"

"To save lives," the professor responded quickly, returning to his lecture.

A few minutes later, the pre-med student spoke up again.

"So how does physics save lives?" he persisted.

"It usually keeps the idiots like you out of medical school," explained the professor.

The Scrounging Maneuver

In a dangerous situation, you must:

- Secure more resources

The sources of resources can be short-term and even short-sighted, but scrounging is preferable to abandoning a move before it pays off when you are heavily invested in it.

Advances should be abandoned for only two reasons:

- The opening has closed.
- It's not worth **future** resources.

At any point in the move, what you have invested thus far are "sunk costs." You cannot get them back whether you give up or not. The only costs that matter are those from now on. You do not quit a difficult journey three feet from a gold mine because your money ran out.

Get more resources any way you can to finish what you started.

MOVE

76
Does This Look Too Tight?

Toward the end of a move, conditions can tighten up. Your resources run low. You have fewer and fewer options as to where to turn. The last stretch is the bridge between success and failure. The shortness of this stretch creates vulnerability.

Tight conditions can easily become a trap. At this late stage, your opponents are likely to know what you are trying to achieve. Because you have so few options, these rivals have a good idea about where they can block you. As your window of opportunity closes, this is when you are at your weakest.

The Surprise Maneuver

Strategists prepare surprises in advance.

In tight situations, you must use cunning to catch your opponents off guard. They know what you have to do. This knowledge is their weakness. You must use it against them. You can surprise them in two ways:

- With extremely secret moves
- With novel unexpected moves

Sneaking By

If you can sneak past, around, or through the opposition, you can escape these tight situations. This relies totally on your being able to move without giving yourself away.

Squeaking By

Coming up with moves that no one else can foresee is much more difficult. You have to rely on:

- The unique features of your situation
- Your opponents' myopic perspective
- Leveraging their assumptions against them

Surprise works because the situation includes a lot of variables people take for granted. Your opponents don't know all your options, all your resources, all your knowledge, and every possible change in climate. Out of these pieces, you can craft a surprise that appears to be one thing but is really something quite different.

A woman asked for the loan officer in a New York bank and explained that she was going to Hong Kong on business for two weeks and needed to borrow $5,000. The loan officer said the bank needed some kind of security for the loan, so the woman gave them the keys and title to a Rolls-Royce parked outside.

The bank agreed to accept the car as collateral and parked the car in the bank's underground lot for safekeeping. The bank's president and officers had a good laugh at the woman for using a $350,000 Rolls as collateral for a $5,000 loan.

Two weeks later, the woman returned and repaid the $5,000 plus the interest, which came to $15.41. The loan officer said, "Miss, this transaction has worked out very nicely, but we are puzzled. While you were away, we found that you are a millionaire. Why would you bother to borrow $5,000?"

The blonde replied, "Where else in New York could I park my car for two weeks for only $15.41 and expect it to be there when I got back?"

77 The Inspiration of Desperation

How bad can a move get? It gets dangerous when your funds run out and opponents multiply against you. Then it gets tight as your options narrow and opponents close in. Finally, these conditions get desperate:

- ☑ Your resources are virtually gone.
- ☑ Your opponents have left you no options.
- ☑ Your situation gets worse every moment.

If you had a time machine, maybe you would go back and never start down this road, but you don't have a time machine. You do have one final maneuver.

The Battle Maneuver

People think that strategy teaches you how to fight people, but the opposite is true. Strategy is about how to avoid fights with people. Conflict is expensive and ideally avoided. Unfortunately, when you are in a desperate condition your only choice is to threaten conflict. Notice, you *threaten* conflict. You don't actually start the conflict, but you ready yourself to go down fighting.

Battle means meeting an opponent or challenge. It means that you have to:

- Put all your resources on the line
- Directly challenge your opponents
- Threaten as much damage as you can

In desperate situations, this is not an emotional reaction but a logical one. Your goal is to get opponents to back down, or, if they won't, beat them in a fight. If you aren't comfortable using extreme action, you must question whether or not you are really in a desperate condition. If you have other options, your situation is just dangerous or tight.

Necessity Is a Mother

When I was diagnosed with cancer, I was in my first truly desperate situation. Until then, each year of my life had been better than the last, but no winning streak goes on forever.

Fortunately, the decision-making skills I had learned in studying strategy served me well. I found out my options and chose an aggressive, quick, painful, and disabling form of treatment. Though the course was far from certain, I was fortunate: I survived. As I went through treatment, I saw other patients die because they were unwilling to make the tough choices.

It was at that point that I realized I needed to teach people how strategy works and why they need its skills to face their problems.

Threatening battle when you are willing to take others down with you can be the key to your success. When you recognize that it is all or nothing at all, you become totally focused.

When you take a desperate stance, it can scare some opponents away. If you threaten them with enough damage, they may well decide that it is not worth fighting you. When your opponents do not back down, you must fight with everything you have.

"Desperate affairs require desperate remedies."
Horatio Nelson

78
Never Give a Sucker an Even Break

First, let us get this clear: conflict is destructive. Strategy means building up positions, not tearing down opponents. Conflict hurts your position as well as your opponents. It is evil.

In modern life, conflict usually takes the form of hostile confrontations. You only engage in these battles in desperate situations when they are unavoidable. Your goal is to secure a position, not to beat up or hurt an opponent. The more you beat up an opponent, the more reasons that opponent has to damage you.

When you are forced to go to battle, you must do everything you can to avoid the destruction of real conflict. This means only one thing.

> THE KEY TO CONFLICT: **When forced to threaten conflict, make it an unfair fight.**

MOVE

Win the Battle Before the Fight

If you pick the conditions of battle, you dramatically increase your chances of success. Before the battle, you can:

- Pick the right place
- Arrange the observers
- Leverage emotions
- Pick the right time
- Make the exit strategy visible
- Make the stakes visible

Make It Hard to Fight

Get the environment on your side. You plan the confrontation in a place that is familiar and comfortable for you, but strange and uncomfortable for your opponent. You gather and prepare your supporters and cut off your opponent's supporters.

Strategists do their opponents a favor by taking away their strength.

Get emotion on your side. You then do everything you can do to confuse your opponent's emotions while you remain calm. You set up the confrontation for late in the day, when your opponent is tired and rushed, but when you have had time to rest and relax.

Make It Easy to Agree

At the beginning of the confrontation, make it clear that you have no way out, but that your opponent does. You are willing to sacrifice everything. Your opponent only has to concede the point in contention.

Readily and quickly concede every good point your opponent has. Look for points of agreement to give your opponent a way to save face in the battle.

This is like going "all in" in Texas Hold'em when you have a weak hand. You push in all your chips before your opponent has too much invested in the pot. You are willing to leave the game if you lose. You want to make the stakes so high that your opponents don't want to play.

79 The Turning of the Tide

You can set up the best conditions for a confrontation, but you cannot control what happens during it. Strategy was designed for unpredictable, contested environments. Battles are:

- Chaotic, progressing without a pattern
- Confusing because it is unclear what is happening
- Fluid, where positions constantly change

Changing the Momentum

You cannot control the battle, but you can control momentum. As we said earlier, momentum doesn't define a steady state of progress but a sudden change in people's expectations. In other words:

Use surprise to change the perception of battle.

In politics, for example, candidates win momentum anytime they do better than expected. If a candidate was expected to lose a debate but does better than expected, that candidate comes out of the debate with more momentum despite the technical loss.

Alternating Battle and Surprise

Surprise is doing the unexpected, the maneuver used under limited conditions. Battle is meeting opponents directly, used under desperate conditions, but:

- Battle is never used without surprise
- Prepare surprises before to use during battle

You are prepared for surprise and your opponents are not. Battle is all emotion because there is very little solid information. When you unleash a surprise, you know what is happening but your opponent doesn't.

Timing and Momentum

Because momentum controls perceptions, you must set up a surprise and release it at the right time for it to be effective.

- You start the battle exactly as expected.
- You use surprise when it will decide the contest.

You start the battle so that your opponent thinks he or she knows what is going on. The battle builds up tension. When the tension gets to the breaking point, you unleash your surprise.

If you time the surprise correctly, it frees your opponent from his or her desire to continue the fight.

"THE WORLD IS WIDE, AND I WILL NOT WASTE MY LIFE IN FRICTION WHEN IT COULD BE TURNED INTO MOMENTUM." FRANCES WILLARD

80
The Keys to Moving

- Be prepared and eager to move instantly when you spot the right opportunity.
- Adapt your moves to instantly adjust to changing situations.
- When you cannot defend your position against attack, divert your opponent from coming after you.
- When moving is easy, keep moving.
- In contests with rivals, get close and block them.
- When the race is on, follow the leader.
- When you are both in the same boat, make temporary alliances with strangers.
- When the going gets tough, you don't have to be tough; you just have to keep going.
- When your options look limited, you can invent whole new options.
- If you are desperate, you can still win the battle by knowing how to discourage a fight.

Part VI
Claim to Harvest the Opportunity

81
Getting Rewarded Is Child's Play

As a psychological and practical matter, you must claim to get rewarded. A reward is the only proof that what you are doing makes sense. If you lose weight and still think you are fat, nothing is won. If you save your company money but nobody knows, you will not get rewarded.

Think **big**. Think long-term. Learn to claim.

A claim is an outward, visible sign that gets you the benefit from change. Change is nothing in itself. It is what you get out of change that matters.

Claiming a Reward

To claim your reward at the end of an advance—especially moves at the end of a campaign—you must:

- Identify the value of your new position
- Think about how to best package your position
- Do the work to get the necessary recognition
- Answer the demands of the position

CLAIM

The Emotional Battle

Claim is not as complicated as the earlier steps in the Progress Cycle, but it is the most emotionally demanding. It requires:

- ☑ Recognizing your failures
- ☑ Asking others to recognize your successes

Demanding Attention

From childhood, we learn to get what we want from our parents. However, as children, we know that our parents notice us, think about us, and will forgive our enthusiasm for recognition.

A small boy was sent up to bed by his father. Five minutes later, the boy called downstairs, "Da-ad?"

"What?" called the father.

"I'm thirsty. Can you get me a drink of water?" asked the boy.

"No, you had your chance. Lights out!" called the father.

Five minutes later, a small voice called again, "Da-aaaad..."

"What?" snapped the father.

"I can't sleep without a drink of water," called the little boy.

"I told you no!" yelled the father. "And if you ask me again, I'll have to come up there and spank you!"

Five minutes later."Daaaa-aaaad..."

"Now what?"

"When you come up to spank me, can you bring a drink of water?"

Unfortunately, we live in a different world as adults than we do as children. You must have the courage to deal with the fact that:

- People do not notice you unless you make them
- People do not take care of you without a reason
- People will not applaud every time you take a bow

"THE POINT IS TO DEVELOP THE CHILDLIKE INCLINATION FOR PLAY AND THE CHILDLIKE DESIRE FOR RECOGNITION AND TO GUIDE THE CHILD OVER TO IMPORTANT FIELDS FOR SOCIETY." ALBERT EINSTEIN

82
Was the Operation a Success?

When you first take aim at an opportunity, you have some idea of how your actions can create a more rewarding position. After you take action, you must evaluate the results of your move. Each strategic advance is an experiment. You can only get the results after you conduct the experiment.

Your New Position

- Have you found a common cause with others?
- Have you gained more responsibility and authority?
- Have you changed how people see the future?
- Have you increased people's trust in you?
- Have you developed more skills and relationships?

The Value of Your New Position

The goal of strategy is to make advances pay. You need to think about the value that the position generates:

How does your new position create value for others?

How can you translate that value into value for yourself?

- Economic value that physically supports you
- Professional value that enhances your uniqueness
- Philosophical value that provides broader perspective

CLAIM

An engineer had a rare gift for fixing complex systems. After working for the same company loyally for over thirty years, he happily retired. Years later his company had a problem with a multimillion-dollar system installed at its biggest customer's site. The company had tried everything and everyone to get the system working, but nothing worked. In desperation, they called on the retired engineer.

The engineer reluctantly took on the challenge. He spent only a couple of hours examining the complex system and then put a small "x" in chalk on a specific component.

"Replace it," he told his former company.

They replaced the part and the system worked perfectly.

A few days later, the company received a bill for $1,000,000 from the engineer. The company was outraged and demanded a complete itemized accounting of the charges.

The engineer sent them the detail.

Two hours of time	$300.00
Placing of chalk mark	$1.00
Knowing where to place it	$999,699.00

When Experiments Fail

All moves are experiments. Many fail to bring us any closer to a reward. You must:

- Never falsely claim success
- Never defend losing positions

You must:

- Put your failures behind you
- Abandon losing positions quickly

THE KEY TO RECOVERY: **You must learn from mistakes.**

The only real failure is not admitting failure.

CLAIM

83
THE GIFT THAT KEEPS ON GIVING

Controlling perceptions is especially important at the end of the process. You must consider other people's viewpoints.

A senator died and St. Peter greeted her in heaven. "Welcome, but we rarely see politicians here so you need to spend time in both heaven and hell so you can decide where you belong."

"Already made up my mind; heaven it is," said the senator.

"Sorry, but heaven has its rules," said St. Peter sadly, putting her on the elevator to hell. "We'll see you soon."

In hell, the senator found herself on a luxurious golf course. At the club, her political friends greeted her in beautiful clothes. They dined on lobster and caviar and told her how well politicians were treated in hell. The Devil joined them, and everyone had such a great time that, before she knew it, she had to leave.

Up in heaven, the senator joined a group of strangers happily singing the praises of God. Heaven was very beautiful, and the people were very nice, but the hours did seem to drag a bit.

When time was up, St. Peter said, "Well, you've seen both hell and heaven. Now, you must choose where to spend eternity."

After some thought, she said, "Heaven is delightful, but I would be happier in hell with my friends and familiar pastimes."

So St. Peter escorted her to the elevator, and down she went.

As the elevator door opened, she smelled a horrible stench. The land was a burning garbage heap covered in half-dead people, writhing in torment. Her friends cried when they saw her.

"I don't understand," stammered the senator to the Devil. "Yesterday, it was all so beautiful. Now it's a nightmare."

The Devil looked at her, smiled, and explained, "I thought you understood. Yesterday was the campaign. Today you voted for us."

Packaging the Results

When it comes time to make a claim, a little effort spent in thinking about appearances goes a long way. You need to do this if only for yourself. People judge by symbols. Words lend meaning. How you describe and represent your accomplishments changes the way you and other people relate to those accomplishments.

THE KEY OF PACKAGING: **Everyone judges the value of work by the care spent in packaging it.**

You may see the value of your new position, but you also need to help other people understand that value. You want a package that:

- People will notice
- Creates a perception of value
- People will care about

Strategy teaches you how to strengthen your position.

If you treat your position and accomplishments as though they don't matter, others will treat them the same way as well. If you treat them as though they are valuable and important, it will increase the value of that position in the eyes of other people. You are humble after you are recognized. You must get attention first.

84
The Greatest Show on Earth

If you need people to recognize your new position before you can be rewarded for it, you must do more than package your new position. You must promote it. People hear only what they want to hear. It is real work to get people to hear what you are saying.

THE KEY TO ATTENTION: **Reverse momentum by getting attention first, then explaining.**

Use surprise to get people's attention.

Use best practices to communicate your message.

Good communication requires first getting people's attention.

David got a parrot as a birthday present, but this bird had a bad attitude and an embarrassing vocabulary. David tried to discourage the bird's swearing, but nothing worked. The more he taught a polite vocabulary, the more the bird swore. The worse David punished the bird, the worse the animal's language became.

Finally, in a moment of desperation, David put the bird in the freezer. At first, the bird screamed expletives and then, suddenly, all was quiet. David was worried that he might have hurt the bird and quickly opened the freezer door.

The parrot calmly stepped onto David's hand and said: "I'm sorry about my language and stubbornness. Please forgive me."

David wanted to ask what had changed the bird when the parrot continued, "May I ask what the chicken did?"

Lights, Camera, Action!

After you get people's attention, you still need to amplify your message to get people to hear you. The rules are:

- Visual communication is more powerful than words.
- The message must suit changing conditions.
- You must send everyone a consistent message.
- Tailor that message to individual self-interest.

Memorable communication requires a touch of drama. Most changes in position are not dramatic in themselves. You can dramatize a new position by creating a visual symbol for the change. Pictures, trophies, and other signs of change are remembered.

- Play it up when ignored.
- Play it down when honored.

Strategy means mastering special communication skills.

Any method of communication gets old and tired. As conditions change, you must continually adjust your communication to contrast it with the conditions. In loud environments, you speak quietly to get attention. In quiet environments, you speak loudly. In dark, you use light. In light, you use shadow.

You cannot send mixed messages. If you tell different stories to different people, it will come back to haunt you.

The only way you can tailor your message is to the particular self-interest of your listener. For a group, you address your message to the group's shared mission. For individuals, you address your message to each person's unique position.

CLAIM

85
Use the Power or Lose the Power

Rather than end with a quote, let us start with one:

> "In theory, there is no difference between theory and practice; In practice, there is." Chuck Reid

Strategy is great in theory but better in practice.

Strategy is meant to be practiced. As the lazy person's route to success, it is designed to get the most out of work, but it only eliminates work if you work it.

Getting value out of a position is work. If you don't use the advantages of a new position, you lose that position. Moving to a better position is like buying a beautiful, fertile field. If you don't till the field, plant it, and harvest it, it turns into a pile of weeds.

Building up Positions

CLAIM

The more you use a position, the more you:

- Learn about the ground
- Understand the trends of climate
- Win command of your situation
- Master the skills of reaping rewards

As you make progress in all these areas, your new position returns more rewards, serving your mission.

Defending Your Position

The better you grow at using your position, the easier it is to defend your position.

- You have more financial resources.
- You get more professional respect.
- You prove the value of your philosophy.

Returning Diminishing Returns

However, over time, if you keep working your position in the same way, you get less and less out of it over time.

- Your place is completed by your work on it.
- Your work gets better, but the place gets poorer.
- What was once rewarding grows emptier.

After awhile, "best practices" become routine and stale. Doing the same things in the same way drains the life out of positions. The fertile field produces less. The rich mine is played out.

The solution, of course, is another advance, which:

- Starts with best practice or your current position
- Then adds innovation or doing something surprising

Every position that is taken for granted is lost. Trouble in your job, in your marriage, or in your life arises because you forget to keep advancing your position.

> "THAT WHICH IS STATIC AND REPETITIVE IS BORING. THAT WHICH IS DYNAMIC AND RANDOM IS CONFUSING. IN BETWEEN LIES ART." JOHN A. LOCKE

Strategic claims open up new areas to exploration.

CLAIM

86
A Good Book Has No Ending

Every ending is a new beginning.

People think that when their dreams come true everything in their lives will be perfect. They cannot enjoy what they have because their minds are filled with "if only's."

- If only I could get that promotion...
- If only my loved one would marry me...
- If only I had children...

However, whenever they get any of these things, they don't find themselves in a state of nirvana. Instead they discover:

> THE KEY TO DREAMS: **When your dreams come true, your problems are just beginning.**

You *do* make progress. Dreams *do* come true, but inside every gift we are given (or we take), there is a new situation ready to challenge us. No matter how far you go, there you are.

CLAIM

No Guarantees and No Limitations

As you meet the next challenge, failure is always a possibility, but you cannot let this knowledge paralyze you. You can never completely protect yourself against failure, but the uncertainty of the future has an upside. Your next advance may turn out to be more rewarding than you can possibly imagine.

You must always be prepared:

- To embrace unforeseen levels of success

- To withstand unforeseen levels of failure

If you are ready for one, you must be equally ready for the other. Neither the costs nor the payoffs in life are predictable. Your fear and greed must balance themselves out in the equation of strategy.

In Every Case

As you move from what you know into areas in which you have a lot to learn, you should expect to fail, but there is a certain joy in "failing forward." Exploring a new area, trying a new thing, and making a good play, even if they don't always work, are more satisfying than watching life pass you by.

Embrace Success

No matter how deep it sounds, the journey is *not* the reward. Everyone is on a journey. Some rise; others fall. Some are having a lot of fun. Many aren't having very much fun at all.

Success comes from continually making progress. Especially when we bring others with us.

THE KEY TO FUN: **Using strategy in the game makes it all more fun—win, lose, or draw.**

As a strategist, you don't care where you start. Each new start and each step forward is rewarding, if only for the change of scenery.

87
The Keys to Claiming

- Return to your childish enthusiasm and innocence and ask for what you want.
- Accept your failures and do not imagine or represent them as successes.
- Learn from your failures but put them behind you as quickly as possible.
- Frame the advantages of your new position so both you and others can easily understand it.
- When you need recognition from others to get rewarded, get their attention first.
- Develop and work your new position to get the most out of it and defend it over time.
- Expect every advance to lead to new challenges.
- The fun is in constantly making progress.

Part VII The Key Is Your Future

88
The Keys and the Golden Key

After my classes, attendees frequently say how obvious strategy is when someone lays it out in a sensible way. But strategy is far from obvious. Our instincts and training work against the uncommon sense of strategy. The forty-six key principles in the previous eighty-seven lessons give you what few people on earth have: a vocabulary for thinking about and discussing strategic situations.

These rules can be overwhelming, but all these lessons and key principles come down to one thing: seeing your place in the world clearly. This perspective is *the* golden key to strategy that is the real topic of this book. Ordinary people see what happens in their lives as complex and confusing. *The Golden Key* makes sense of it all, putting everything in perspective.

The Whole Is More Than Its Parts

On first reading, this book opens your mind. On rereading, its lessons grow more powerful because the connections become more important than the parts. You don't have to memorize all these rules. Once you see how they fit together as a whole and grasp the whole system, you can throw away the rules.

The Story Thus Far

All the key principles in this book, taken together, tell a story about how the world works and why it works that way. Instead of listing the rules over again, let us end by telling the whole story in a few paragraphs. If we had started with this story, it wouldn't have made much sense because you didn't have the right vocabulary, but after reading this book, you should understand what all these words really mean in the context of strategy.

Strategy lights the way to a new and better place.

The HIGHLIGHTED words are the names of our key principles in the same order they appear in the book.

Strategy

Strategy is a system to ADVANCE your position over time. INSTINCT forces people to damage their position under pressure because they don't know what to do. Your position exists both in the physical environment and in people's PERCEPTION of you.

Five dimensions define your POSITION. MISSION is the core purpose that drives you and unites you with others. GROUND is where you compete and where your reward comes from. CLIMATE describes the changes that you cannot control. COMMAND is how your character affects your decision-making. SYSTEMS are your skills in working with others.

Every aspect of the world is made of COMPLEMENTARY OPPOSITES. The natural shift between these opposites creates openings for new OPPORTUNITIES. These changes result in the constant CREATION of new positions and DESTRUCTION of existing positions.

Progress

SUCCESS means advancing your position in rewarding ways. You advance with the four steps in THE PROGRESS CYCLE using their constant REPETITION. SCALABILITY breaks each step down into easier cycles. CAMPAIGNS of multiple advances are necessary to surmount obstacles. LISTENING alerts you to opportunities. To AIM, you must decide what to do and what not to do. When you decide, you must MOVE to take your commitments to completion. In the end, you must CLAIM to get the rewards of your new position.

Listen

ASKING questions gets others working for you. You must overcome SELECTIVE HEARING to understand their answers. Conditions change through REVERSAL. You can understand the complex conditions in your environment through SIMPLIFICATION, reducing them all to either "empty" or "full." INVERSION creates OPENINGS in empty places that you can fill. You use SECRECY to protect your knowledge. You CONTROL others by knowing more than they do.

Aim

You choose tasks that you can accomplish with EASE. LESS IS MORE when it comes to choosing tasks. You develop MOMENTUM by combining what people expect with the unexpected. You use DEFENSE to protect an existing position while making a DECISION about the best advance defined by the principles of PARSIMONY. OPPORTUNISM uses openings while PREPARATION assures moves will get rewarded.

Move

You must avoid creating RESISTANCE from others as you move forward, using ADAPTABILITY to instantly adjust to your specific situation. When you come into CONFLICT with others, you must make it an unfair fight to discourage them.

Claim

To make a RECOVERY, you must recognize your mistakes, but you must use PACKAGING to clearly define your success. You must demand ATTENTION when you want others to reward you. When your DREAMS come true, your challenges are just beginning, but using strategy makes working through them more FUN than anything.

The Final Key

No matter how far strategy takes you, you always have this...

> THE KEY TO HAPPINESS:
>
> **Happiness is looking forward to the coming attractions.**

It's life's Swiss Army knife!

Strategy is the universal tool for meeting challenges.

About the Author

Gary Gagliardi is a successful entrepreneur, a strategic trainer, a news analyst, and the award-winning author of over a dozen books on strategy, adapting its principles to every aspect of modern life. Visit **BooksOnStrategy.com** to learn more about his books and seminar programs.

"Everything you've learned in school as 'obvious' becomes less and less obvious as you begin to study the universe." R. Buckminster Fuller